WORLD WAR II FROM ORIGINAL SOURCES

THE BATTLE OF THE BULGE

THE FIRST EIGHT DAYS

EDITED AND INTRODUCED BY BOB CARRUTHERS

Pen & Sword
MILITARY

This edition published in 2013 by
Pen & Sword Military
An imprint of
Pen & Sword Books Ltd
47 Church Street
Barnsley
South Yorkshire
S70 2AS

First published in Great Britain in 2011 in digital format by Coda Books Ltd.

ISBN 978 1 78159 142 0

Originally published as part of the US Army in Action series, as 'Bastogne - the Story of the First Eight Days In Which the 101st Airborne Division Was Closed Within the Ring of German Forces' in Washington, D.C. Infantry journal Press, 1946. Written by Colonel S. L. A. Marshall, and assisted by Captain John G. Westover And Lieutenant A. Joseph Webber (Drawings By Technical Sergeant Olin Dows)

A CIP catalogue record for this book is available from the British Library

Printed and bound by
CPI Group (UK) Ltd, Croydon, CR0 4YY

Pen & Sword Books Ltd incorporates the Imprints of Pen & Sword Aviation, Pen & Sword Family History, Pen & Sword Maritime, Pen & Sword Military, Pen & Sword Discovery, Pen & Sword Politics, Pen & Sword Atlas, Pen & Sword Archaeology, Wharncliffe Local History, Wharncliffe True Crime, Wharncliffe Transport, Pen & Sword Select, Pen & Sword Military Classics, Leo Cooper, The Praetorian Press, Claymore Press, Remember When, Seaforth Publishing and Frontline Publishing

For a complete list of Pen & Sword titles please contact
PEN & SWORD BOOKS LIMITED
47 Church Street, Barnsley, South Yorkshire, S70 2AS, England
E-mail: enquiries@pen-and-sword.co.uk
Website: www.pen-and-sword.co.uk

CONTENTS

INTRODUCTION

There are few better accounts of the first eight days of the Battle of the Bulge than S.L.A. Marshall's excellent account of the events as viewed from the US perspective. This masterful study was first published in 1946 and appeared in the Infantry Journal Inc, but was rescued from obscurity by the programme of reprints undertaken by the Center For Military History.

Marshall's study is definitely "of its time" and was written when the memories of the events were still fresh. The attitudes expressed by Marshall reflect the prevailing mood of the immediate post-war era. To a modern audience the tone might feel jingoistic, and to an extent even boastful, but in many respects that is what makes them so interesting today. This is an account of the fighting expressed in the language of the day by those who were there on the ground. It reflects their pride in their achievements and provides a modern audience with a unique insight into the attitude towards events which had so recently unfolded.

I hope you enjoy this book and will join us in exploring others in the series.

Bob Carruthers

FOREWORD

The Center of Military History is pleased to present the second volume in the U.S. Army in Action series, a facsimile reprint of Brigadier General S. L. A. Marshall's Bastogne: The First Eight Days. Originally published in 1946, this brief study provides a combat history of a critical battle during the Allied liberation of Europe in World War II. Outnumbered and surrounded for five days, a U.S. Army combined arms force of airborne infantry, armor, engineers, tank destroyers, and artillery conducted a successful defense of the Belgian crossroads town of Bastogne in late December 1944. They separated the German combined arms formations and destroyed the pieces, halting the offensive. The outcome of this battle was critical to the successful Allied defense against the German Ardennes offensive.

Bastogne offers unique insights, capturing the immediate impressions of the soldiers who fought in this harsh winter engagement. The author penetrates the "fog of war" with a coherent narrative that clearly captures the strategy, tactics, and leadership of the battle. This action strangled the German logistical flow to their forward assault divisions, disrupting their offensive tempo and slowing their advance. What emerges is a vivid case study of how decisive leadership and incidents of individual heroism can contribute to overcoming enemy forces and weather.

Historians and professional soldiers will find Bastogne a valuable addition to their reading list. The Center of Military History recommends it highly for use in conjunction with Staff Rides. Although later studies provide more depth of research and detailed analysis concerning the Battle of Bastogne, Marshall's book, with its excellent maps, provides a superb one-volume narrative which can be utilized as a guide for officers and noncommissioned officers when visiting the Ardennes battlefield.

The Center wishes to thank Mrs. S.L.A. Marshall for her kind assistance with our efforts to reprint Bastogne as well as her continued support of the U.S. Army Historical Programs.

WASHINGTON, D.C.
WILLIAM A. STOFFT
Brigadier General,. U.S. Army
Chief of Military History

UNITS, COMMANDERS, STAFF MEMBERS, AND MEMBERS OF UNITS MENTIONED IN THIS NARRATIVE

HIGHER UNITS

SHAEF (Supreme Headquarters Allied Expeditionary Forces)
Commanding General: General of the Army Dwight D. Eisenhower
Chief of Staff: Lt. Gen. Walter B. Smith
A. C. of S., G-3: Maj. Gen. J. F. M. Whiteley

12TH ARMY GROUP
Commanding General: Gen. Omar N. Bradley

FIRST ARMY
Commanding General: Gen. Courtney H. Hodges

THIRD ARMY
Commanding General: Lt. Gen. George S. Patton, Jr.

VIII CORPS
Commanding General: Maj. Gen. Troy H. Middleton

XVIII CORPS (Airborne)
Commanding General: Maj. Gen. Matthew B. Ridgway
Acting Commander at the beginning of the Bastogne concentration: Maj. Gen. James M. Gavin
Chief of Staff: Colonel Ralph D. Eaton

THE BASTOGNE FORCES

101st AIRBORNE DIVISION
Commanding General: Maj. Gen. Maxwell D. Taylor
Acting Division Commander during the first phase of Bastogne operations: Brig. Gen. Anthony C. McAuliffe
Assistant Division Commander: Brig. Gen. Gerald J. Higgins
A. C. of S., G-1, and Acting Chief of Staff: Lt. Col. Ned D. Moore

A. C. of S., G-2: Lt. Col. Paul A. Danahy
A. C. of S., G-3: Lt. Col. H. W. O. Kinnard
A. C. of S., GA Lt. Col. Carl W. Kohls
Surgeon: Lt. Col. David Gold
Civil Affairs Officer: Capt. Robert S. Smith
Aide to the Commanding General: Lt. Frederic D. Starrett
Division Artillery Commander: Col. Thomas L. Sherburne, Jr.

501ST PARACHUTE INFANTRY REGIMENT
Commanding Officer: Lt. Col. Julian J. Ewell
S-4: Maj. William H. Butler
1ST BATTALION (Companies A, B, C and Hq.)
Commanding Officer: Major Raymond V. Bottomly, Jr.
2D BATTALION (Companies D, E, F and Hq.)
Commanding Officer: Major Sammie N. Homan
3D BATTALION (Companies G, H, I and Hq.)
Commanding Officer: Lt. Col. George A Griswold
Members of this regiment who figure in the narrative:
Company A Capt. Stanfield A. Stach; Lt. James C. Murphy; Lt. Joseph B.
Schweiker; Sgt. Lyle B. Chamberlain; Pfc. William C. Michel
Company D: Cpl. Frank Lasik; Pvt. Manzi

502D PARACHUTE INFANTRY REGIMENT
Commanding Officer: Lt. Col. Steve A. Chappuis
Executive: Lt. Col. Patrick J. Cassidy
S-3: Capt. James J. Hatch
Surgeon: Major Douglas T. Davidson
Commander, Hq. Co.: Capt. James C. Stone
1ST BATTALION (Companies A, B, C and Hq.)
Commanding Officer: Major John D. Hanlon
S-2: Lt. Samuel B. Nickels, Jr.
Company A Capt. Wallace A. Swanson
Company C: Capt. George R. Cody.
2D BATTALION (Companies D, E, F and Hq.)
Commanding Officer: Lt. Col. Thomas H. Sudiffe
3D BATTALION (Companies G, H, I and Hq.)
Commanding Officer: Lt. Col. John P. Stopka

506TH PARACHUTE INFANTRY REGIMENT

Commanding Officer: Col. Robert F. Sink

S-4: Capt. Salve H. Matheson

1ST BATTALION (Companies A, B, C and Hq.)

Commanding Officer: Lt. Col. James L. LaPrade

Commanding Officer (after Col. LaPrade was killed in action): Major Robert F. Harwick

Commanding Officer (after Major Harwick was wounded in action): Lt. Col. Robert L. Strayer

2D BATTALION (Companies D, E, F and Hq.)

Commanding Officer: Lt. Col. Robert L. Strayer

Commanding Officer (after Col. Strayer took over 1st Battalion): Major Lloyd E. Patch

3D BATTALION (Companies G, H, I and Hq.)

Commanding Officer: Major Gus M. Heilman

327TH GLIDER INFANTRY REGIMENT

Commanding Officer: Col. Joseph H. Harper

Executive: Lt. Col. Thomas J. Rouzie

1ST BATTALION (Companies A, B, C and Hq.)

Commanding Officer: Lt. Col. Hartford F. Salee

2D BATTALION (Companies E, F, G and Hq.)

Commanding Officer: Lt. Col. Roy L. Inman

Executive (and Commanding Officer, following the wounding of Col. Inman): Major R. B. Galbreaith

3D BATTALION (Companies A, B, C and Hq.)

Note: Though carried as the 3d Battalion, 327th Glider Infantry, in this narrative, and considered such by the command, this battalion was actually the 1st Battalion, 401st Glider Infantry, which accounts for the presence within the one regiment of two battalions with A-B-C letter companies. This battalion had served as the 3d Battalion of the regiment since the Normandy landing.

Commanding Officer: Lt, Col. Ray C. Allen

Members of this regiment who figure in the narrative:

Company F: Capt. James F. Adams; Lt. Leslie E. Smith; Tech. Sgt. Oswald Y. Butler; Staff Sgt. Carl E. Dickinson.

Company G: Capt. Hugh Evans; Lt. Stanley A. Morrison

Company A, 3d Battalion: Lt. Howard G. Bowles

Company B, 3d Battalion: Capt. Robert J. McDonald; Tech. Sgt. Mike

Campano

Company C, 3d Battalion: Capt. Preston E. Towns

321ST GLIDER FIELD ARTILLERY BATTALION

Commanding Officer: Lt. Col. Edward L. Carmichael

907th GLIDER FIELD ARTILLERY BATTALION

Commanding Officer: Lt. Col. Clarence F. Nelson

377TH PARACHUTE FIELD ARTILLERY BATTALION

Commanding Officer: Lt. Col. Harry W. Elkins

463D PARACHUTE FIELD ARTILLERY BATTALION

Commanding Officer: Lt. Col. John T. Cooper, Jr.

81ST AIRBORNE ANTIAIRCRAFT BATTALION

Commanding Officer: Lt. Col. X. B. Cox, Jr.

326TH AIRBORNE ENGINEER BATTALION

Commanding Officer: Lt. Col. Hugh A. Mozley

426TH AIRBORNE QUARTERMASTER COMPANY

Commanding Officer: Capt. George W. Horn

101st AIRBORNE SIGNAL COMPANY

Commanding Officer: Capt. William J. Johnson

801ST AIRBORNE ORDNANCE MAINTENANCE COMPANY

Commanding Officer: Capt. John L. Patterson

326TH AIRBORNE MEDICAL COMPANY

Commanding Officer: Major William E. Barfield

ATTACHED UNITS

COMBAT COMMAND B, 10TH ARMORED DIVISION

7015TH TANK DESTROYER BATTALION

755TH FIELD ARTILLERY BATTALION

COMPANY C, 9TH ARMORED ENGINEERS

969TH FIELD ARTILLERY BATTALION

COMBAT COMMAND R (37TH BATTALION), 4TH ARMORED DIVISION

COMPOSITION AND COMMAND OF MAJOR ATTACHED UNITS

COMBAT COMMAND B, 10TH ARMORED DIVISION.

This unit operated independently in conjunction with the 101st Airborne Division until December 21, when it was attached to the 101st and came under its command.

Commanding Officer: Col. William L. Roberts

Combat Command B was divided for tactical purposes into four main parts: the units held directly under the commander, and Teams Cherry, Desobry and O'Hara. The following units of Combat Command B were directly under the commander:

HEADQUARTERS AND HEADQUARTERS COMPANY
3D TANK BATTALION (LESS COMPANY C)
COMPANY C, 21st TANK BATTALION
54TH ARMORED INFANTRY BATTALION (LESS COMPANIES A AND C)
20TH ARMORED INFANTRY BATTALION (LESS COMPANY C)
COMPANY C, 609TH TANK DESTROYER BATTALION (LESS PLATOONS WITH TEAMS)
COMPANY C, 55Th ARMORED ENGINEER BATTALION (LESS PLATOONS WITH TEAMS)
420TH ARMORED FIELD ARTILLERY BATTALION
Commanding Officer: Lt. Col. Barry D. Browne
BATTERY B, 796TH ANTIAIRCRAFT BATTALION
TROOP D, 90TH RECONNAISSANCE (CAVALRY) SQUADRON (LESS PLATOONS WITH TEAMS)

TEAM CHERRY
Commanding Officer: Lt. Col. Henry T. Cherry (also commanding officer of 3d Tank Battalion)
3D TANK BATTALION (LESS COMPANY B AND 2D PLATOON, COMPANY D)
COMPANY A: Lt. Edward P. Hyduke
COMPANY C, 20TH ARMORED INFANTRY BATTALION: Capt. Willis F. Ryerson; Lt. Earl B. Gilligan
3D PLATOON, COMPANY C, 55TH ARMORED ENGINEER BATTALION
ONE PLATOON, COMPANY C, 609TH TANK DESTROYER BATTALION
2D PLATOON, TROOP D, 90TH RECONNAISSANCE SQUADRON

TEAM DESOBRY
Commanding Officer: Major William R. Desobry (also commanding officer, 20th Armored Infantry Battalion). Major Charles L. Hustead took command after Major Desobry was wounded.
20TH ARMORED INFANTRY BATTALION (LESS COMPANIES A AND C)
HEADQUARTERS COMPANY: Capt. Gordon Geiger; Lt. Eugene Todd
COMPANY B: Capt. Omar M. Billett

COMPANY B, 3D TANK BATTALION

ONE PLATOON, COMPANY C, 609TH TANK DESTROYER BATTALION

ONE PLATOON, COMPANY D, 3D TANK BATTALION (LIGHT TANKS)

ONE PLATOON, COMPANY C, 55TH ARMORED ENGINEER BATTALION

ONE PLATOON, COMPANY C, 609TH TANK DESTROYER BATTALION

ONE PLATOON, TROOP D, 90TH RECONNAISSANCE SQUADRON

TEAM O'HARA

Commanding Officer: Lt. Col. James O'Hara (also commanding officer of 54th Armored Infantry Battalion)

S-2: Capt. Edward A. Carrigo

54TH ARMORED INFANTRY BATTALION (LESS COMPANIES A AND C)

COMPANY B: Lt. John D. Devereaux

COMPANY C, 21st TANK BATTALION

ONE PLATOON, COMPANY C, 55TH ARMORED ENGINEER BATTALION

ONE PLATOON, COMPANY D, 3D TANK BATTALION (LIGHT TANKS): Lt. Sherwood D. Wishart

ONE PLATOON, TROOP D, 90TH RECONNAISSANCE SQUADRON

FORCE CHARLIE 16: Lt. Richard C. Gilliland

705th Tank Destroyer Battalion. This unit operated independently in conjunction with the 101st Airborne Division until December 21 when it was attached to the 101st and came under its command.

Commanding Officer: Lt. Col. Clifford D. Templeton

Headquarters Company (less the battalion trains which were ordered to "find a haven in the west")

Reconnaissance Company

Company A (less one platoon detached to guard the road junction at Laroche)

Company B: Lt. Robert Andrews; Lt. Frederick Mallon; Sgt. Floyd A. Johnson; Sgt. George N. Schmidt; Sgt. Darrell J. Lindley

Company C

Ninth Air Force (members of liaison group attached to 101st Airborne Division during Bastogne operation): Capt. James E. Parker; Lt. Gorden O. Rothwell; Sgt. Frank B. Hotard

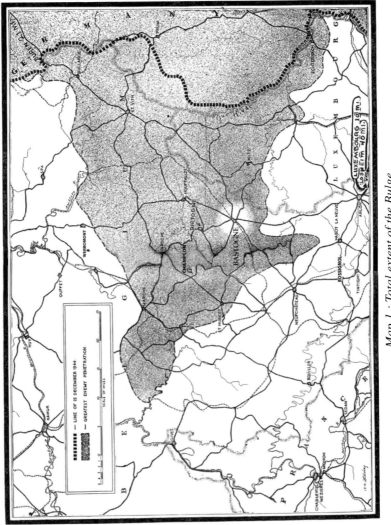

Map 1 : Total extent of the Bulge

1. THE SITUATION

THE SIEGE OF BASTOGNE is one chapter in the history of the battle of the Ardennes. On December 16, 1944, the Germans launched their greatest offensive of the war in the west. Achieving a considerable success in their first attacks, they broke through, penetrated 65 miles into Allied territory, halted the Allied offensive then going on, and threatened the entire front in the west. The failure of this German drive was due in part to the American resistance at St. Vith and Bastogne.

The background of Bastogne dates from the fall of 1944. At that time three American armies, forming the 12th Army Group, were in position on the central part of the western front. The U. S. First and Third Armies were along the Siegfried Line and the U. S. Ninth Army was facing the Roer River in Germany some thirty miles from the Rhine. All three armies were pushing for the Rhine over difficult terrain, across swollen rivers, and against determined enemy resistance. Except in the Aachen sector, where an advance was made to the Roer, the line did not move during October and November. The Third Army fought near Metz; the First and Ninth Armies made their advance farther north, near Aachen. In between these two major efforts the First Army held an extensive line of defense. Of this line the southern and major part was maintained by the U. S. VIII Corps.

On December 16, VIII Corps, under the command of Major General Troy H. Middleton had its headquarters in Bastogne, Belgium. Its area extended from Losheim, Germany, north to a point where the Our River crosses the Franco-German border. Generally parallel to the German frontier along eastern Belgium and Luxembourg, its front was 88 miles wide. The country, the Ardennes, has rugged hills; there are high plateaus, deep-cut valleys and a restricted road net.

The mission that First Army gave VIII Corps was to defend this line in place. New divisions were brought into this part of the front for battle indoctrination, and battle-worn divisions were sent to VIII Corps for re-equipment and rest. As divisions were rotated into the sector, they took over existing wire nets and other facilities.

At the beginning of the German attack in December, the VIII

1. Major Gemeral Troy H. Middleton, Commanding Gerneral, VIII Corps

Corps front was held by two battle-weary divisions, a green infantry division, part of a green armored division, and a cavalry group. The battle-tested divisions (they had both seen months of fighting) were the 4th Infantry Division, which in November had fought a costly action through the Hürtgen Forest below Düren, Germany, and the 28th Infantry Division, which had sustained heavy casualties in the First Army drive to the Roer. The 106th Infantry Division, newly arrived on the Continent, entered the Corps line four days before the German offensive began. The 14th Cavalry Group, consisting of the 18th and 32d Cavalry Squadrons, held the north flank of VIII Corps, and the 9th Armored Division, minus Combat Command B which was with V Corps, had the most of its units attached to the divisions.

The enemy facing the VIII Corps was estimated at four divisions. From north to south these were the 18th, 26th, 352d and 212th. Early in December the 28th Division took prisoners and reaffirmed the presence of the 26th and 352d Divisions, but rumors that one or more panzer units were in rear of these infantry divisions were not confirmed. From December 12 on, the American outposts along the VIII Corps front heard sounds of a great volume of vehicular movement behind the enemy lines.

On the morning of December 16, the VIII Corps front, which had been quiet since the latter part of September, suddenly flared up. For more than a month the enemy had been concentrating some 25 divisions. It had been skillfully done and the extent of the concentration was not fully known to our forces. At 0500 heavy artillery concentrations struck along the entire VIII Corps front and these were soon followed by tank and infantry attacks. The strongest attacks were in the north, near the V and VIII Corps boundary.

The infantry-tank attack on the north flank of the VIII Corps began at 0800 on the 16th, and in three hours the enemy had penetrated the position of the 14th Cavalry group three miles.

Group reserves were committed and the 106th Division put out flank protection to the north. Through the right of the 106th Division the enemy advanced rapidly for a mile and a half, but then as reserves were brought up his progress was slowed. The German gains threatened to isolate two regiments of the 106th Division. Captured documents showed that on this day the enemy hoped to take St. Vith. This he did not do.

Against the 28th Division the enemy used two panzer divisions, three infantry divisions and one parachute division in an infantry-tank attack on the "Ridge Road" just west of the Our River. In this operation, two enemy divisions assaulted each regiment of the 28th. In the center and right of the 28th the enemy made advances up to four and a half miles and crossed the north-south highway at several points. In the southern part of the VIII Corps the 9th Armored and the 4th Infantry Divisions were also attacked by the enemy. These attacks were diversionary to prevent our shifting troops to the north.

At the start of the German offensive the VIII Corps reserve consisted of an armored combat command and four battalions of combat engineers. The engineers were assembled during the first morning, and as the seriousness of the enemy thrust became apparent, additional troops were made available. In the north on December 17, Combat Command R of the 9th Armored Division was released from V Corps and the 7th Armored Division was ordered to close into an assembly area near St. Vith. In the south the 10th Armored Division was moved toward an assembly area near the city of Luxembourg. Orders were also issued to move the 101st and 82d Airborne Divisions to the general area threatened.

From captured documents and from the direction of early thrusts it seemed evident to VIII Corps that the objective of the attacks was Liège and possibly Namur. This, however, was a clear case of VIII Corps misunderstanding the enemy's intent, though the same misunderstanding prevailed in the entire Army for months afterward. It was finally found, however, that Hitler had given his commanders in the Bulge attack specific and inflexible orders to stay to the south of Liège. *[This information is from the European Theater of Operations Historical File of interviews with high-ranking German commanders. It comes from interviews with Colonel General Jodl and Field Marshal Keitel, and is confirmed by all subordinate commanders interviewed.]*

On the 17th, the second day of the offensive, the enemy increased his pressure along the whole front especially in the north. The right flank of V Corps was forced back and in the VIII Corps, German infantry and armor had by 0900 cut off two regiments of the 106th Division. To stem the advance on St. Vith the 168th Engineer Combat Battalion fought a delaying action north and east of that town, Combat Command B of the 9th Armored Division was put into the line, and the 7th Armored Division was committed piecemeal to defensive action as it arrived during the evening.

In the 28th Division sector the Germans began their attacks early and made large gains. The left flank of the 28th was forced to withdraw to the west bank of the Our River and the right was pushed back an additional one to four miles. But it was in the center of the division that the enemy made his deepest penetrations, thrusting one salient of eight miles and another of six. Everywhere the American withdrawal had been four to six miles. At some points the enemy was within 11 miles of Bastogne.

On the southern flank of the VIII Corps the 4th Infantry Division defended against strong attacks, but the enemy did not make the heavy effort here that he had made farther to the north. The 10th Armored Division reached the Luxembourg area in time to assure its defense.

On December 18, the third day of the offensive, the enemy increased the momentum of his drive in the center of VIII Corps.

The Corps north flank was bolstered by the arrival of the 7th Armored Division but remained extremely critical because of the deep German penetrations into the V Corps sector. But the weight against the 28th Division was so overwhelming that its thin defenses disintegrated and the enemy achieved a breakthrough. The right Hank of the 28th, which pulled back across the Our River on the upper eastern border of Luxembourg the previous night, was unable to stabilize its lines. In the withdrawal a wide gap was created through which the enemy pushed a great deal of armor. In the center, enemy thrusts between strongpoints encircled companies and destroyed or captured them one by one. To the 28th Division headquarters the picture was obscure throughout the day because of lost communications, but the appearance of many enemy columns behind the regimental sectors and the tragic tales of stragglers indicated a complete disintegration of regimental defenses. The 28th Division command post itself was attacked when the enemy approached Wiltz. The 44th Engineer Combat Battalion, the 447th Antiaircraft Battalion, and miscellaneous headquarters personnel from the division were used to defend the town. The command post had communications left with only one regiment.

Directly behind the 28th Division, on the St. Vith-Bastogne road, were roadblocks established by the Combat Command Reserve of the 9th Armored Division. One block, known as Task Force Rose, was attacked by the enemy in the morning and was overrun by 1400, December 18. A roadblock on the Wiltz-Bastogne road, known as Task Force Hayze, came under heavy attack by 1815. The Germans overran this roadblock during the night of December 18-19 to come within three kilometers of Bastogne. The defense of Bastogne now became the task of airborne infantry and armored units which had been ordered into the sector.

2. THE CONCENTRATION ON BASTOGNE

O N THE MORNING of December 17 at SHAEF two members of the Supreme General Staff looked at the map and pondered the question of where best to employ SHAEF Reserve, which at that moment consisted of the two American divisions, the 82d Airborne and the 101st Airborne, recently withdrawn from the lines in Holland.

"I think I should put them there," said Major General J. F. M. Whiteley, the Assistant Chief of Staff, G-3, "the place has the best road net in the area."

Lieutenant General W. B. Smith, General Eisenhower's Chief of Staff nodded and said to go ahead and do it. He based his decision purely on the thought of how advantageous Bastogne's radial highway net appeared on the map. It was his idea at the time that both 101st and 82d Airborne Divisions should be employed in the Bastogne area. It was in this way that the Airborne Corps happened to make its start toward Bastogne.

SHAEF's general concept was subsequently modified by decisions made at lower headquarters although the initial impetus had been given in the required direction. The change in direction for the 82d Division, which was to have some of its greatest days in the fighting around Werbomont on the northern flank of the Bulge, came after the XVIII Airborne Corps (82d and 101st Divisions) had passed from SHAEF Reserve into the command of 12th Army Group, which was already forming other plans both for the defense of Bastogne and the employment of the airborne strength. But out of the difference in the SHAEF concept of how to employ the airborne force and the ideas which

Colonel (now Brigadier General) William L. Roberts, Commanding Officer,
Combat Command B, 10th Armoured Division.

were already forming at 12th Army Group there came some early confusion to the two Corps commanders directly concerned and to their forces. However (as later reported in this chapter) the situation was clarified before any real harm was done.

On December 17 and 18, three battle-tested organizations, by different routes and under separate authority, began their moves toward the town in the Belgian Ardennes with whose name their own fame was to be thereafter inseparably linked. Orders from 12th Army Group were received on the 16th directing the 10th Armored Division to be temporarily attached to VIII Corps, First Army, to counter the serious German attempt at a breakthrough. At 1320 on December 17, in compliance with the order, Combat

Major General Maxwell D. Taylor confers with officers of his Division after the Bastogne relief by the 4th Armored Division. They are Major James J. Hatch, 502d Parachute Infantry; Brigadier General Higgins, Assistant Division Commander; and Colonel Robert F. Sink, Commanding Officer, 506th Parachute Infantry.

Command B, 10th Armored Division, took its first step toward Bastogne when it moved from a rest area at Remeling, France, to the vicinity of Merl in Luxembourg.

That evening at 2030 the 101st Airborne Division, which was then re-outfitting in a training area at Camp Mourmelon (near Reims, France, and roughly 100 miles from Bastogne) received telephone orders from Headquarters XVIII Airborne Corps that it was to move north though at that time Bastogne was not the destination given. On the following night, December 18 at 1800, the 705th Tank Destroyer Battalion, then in position at Kohlscheid, Germany (about 60 miles north of Bastogne) was ordered by the Ninth Army to march to Bastogne and report to VIII Corps.

Bastogne, then the Headquarters of VIII Corps, was the natural place for rendezvous and for stabilizing the defense. The town is the hub of the highway net covering the eastern Ardennes - a countryside that is forbidding to the movement of mechanized forces except when the roads are available. By holding at Bastogne the VIII Corps could unhinge the communications of the Germans who were striking west toward the line of the River Meuse.

Combat Command B closed into the vicinity of Merl at 2155 on the 17th. On the following morning it was ordered to move independently of the 10th Armored Division to join VIII Corps. It took the road through Arlon to Bastogne. On the way Colonel William L. Roberts, the commander, received a request from Major General Norman D. Cota, commanding the 28th Infantry Division, to support his force at Wiltz by putting Combat Command B into position south and southeast of the town. But this Colonel Roberts could not do and comply with his Corps orders, so he took his column on into Bastogne and reported there to Major General Middleton at 1600 on the 18th.

At Camp Mourmelon, the 101st Division was short many of its soldiers who were on leave in Paris. The commander of the

Brigadier General (now Major General) Anthony C. McAuliffe, who was Acting Commanding General, 101st Airborne Division, during the first phase of the siege of Bastogne.

XVIII Airborne Corps, Major General Matthew B. Ridgway, was at the rear headquarters of the Corps in England. The 101st Division commander, Major General Maxwell D. Taylor, was in the United States. Upon hearing of the attack and of the fact that the 101st had been committed to battle, he immediately took a plane for Europe. The assistant division commander, Brigadier General Gerald J. Higgins, was giving a lecture in England on the earlier airborne operation in Holland. With him were five of the senior commanders of divisional units and sixteen junior officers. The night would pass before these men were to hear that the division had been alerted for movement to the front and it would be noon of the next day before they were all rounded up and ready to emplane for Mourmelon. So the senior division officer present in France, the artillery commander, Brigadier General Anthony C. McAuliffe, got the division staff together at 2100 on December 17 and outlined the prospect in these words:

"All I know of the situation is that there has been a breakthrough and we have got to get up there."

General McAuliffe directed the Division to move out in combat teams without waiting for the men on pass in Paris or elsewhere to get back. However, the destination of the 101st as given at this time was not Bastogne but Werbomont to the northwest of Bastogne.

At 2030 on the 17th, Lieutenant Colonel Ned D. Moore, Chief of Staff of the 101st, had been called on the telephone by Colonel Ralph D. Eaton, Chief of Staff of the XVIII Corps, and the mission had been outlined in that manner. In moving to Werbomont, the 101st would pass within a short distance of Bastogne and to the westward of it. There was no later modification of this order while 101st remained at Camp Mourmelon.

On the following morning, December 18, the Acting Commander of the XVIII Corps, Major General James M. Gavin, attended a meeting at First Army at which it was decided to attach the 82d Division to the V Corps (since the XVIII Airborne Corps could not move in and become operational until the morning of December 19), and the 101st Division to the VIII Corps. However, no word of this change got down to the 101st Division; throughout that day its staff was unaware either that Bastogne was the destination or that VIII Corps was now their next higher headquarters.

An advance party was then set up to precede the 101st

Brigadier General Gerald J. Higgins, Assistant Division Commander, 101st Airborne Division.

Division to Bastogne. In the party were a representative from each major unit and a company of Engineers who were to be used as guides to lead the combat teams into their Bastogne assembly areas. During the morning of December 18, there had been no time to brief the advance party. Just as the party was pulling away from Camp Mourmelon during the noon hour Colonel Moore ran out of the division command post and advised them that XVIII Corps was to handle the operation and that they should go to a rendezvous with a part of the XVIII Corps staff. They were to meet them at the crossroads in Werbomont. This they did.

General Ridgway arrived at Mourmelon about an hour later, having flown from England. He went to the command post of the 101st and Colonel Moore gave him the situation as he had given it to the advance party. Then occurred an odd sequence of events in which Fate might have played a stronger hand against 101st Division had it not been for several providential circumstances. Ridgway went into General Taylor's empty office and called a higher headquarters - presumably his own Corps. In this conversation he learned that 101st's destination was Bastogne, not Werbomont. On the heels of this conversation, General Higgins entered the room, having just reported from England. Ridgway told him that 101st Division was to go to Bastogne. Ridgway then left Mourmelon for the front. Higgins

Paratroopers entrucking at Camp Mourmelon, France, December 18th 1944, to move to Bastogne.

soon followed. McAuliffe had left an instruction that Higgins was to get forward as rapidly as possible, so he picked a route via Sedan, figuring that it would be less encumbered with traffic. But the word that Bastogne was the Division's destination was not passed to Colonel Moore and the units remained alerted for

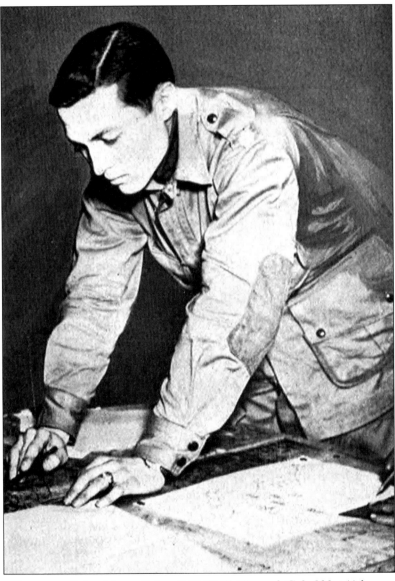

Lieutenant Colonel (now Colonel) H. W. O. Kinnard, G-3, 101st Airborne Division.

movement to Werbomont.

On reaching Werbomont on the night of December 18 the advance party were told that the operation was being handled by VIII Corps and that they were even then due in Bastogne. In this way the advance party failed in its mission and did not reach the objective until 0300 on the morning of December 19. But others were doing their work for them.

Some few minutes before the advance party had left Mourmelon, General McAuliffe had started for Werbomont taking with him his G-3, Lieutenant Colonel H. W. O. Kinnard and his aide, First Lieutenant Frederic D. Starrett. They drove as fast as they could, passing many elements of the 82d Airborne Division along the route. The 82d had been out of the lines in Holland longer than the 101st and was more fully equipped. The 82d was therefore ordered to move out ahead of the 101st. Come to the road juncture south of the Bois de Herbaimont (nine miles northwest of Bastogne) General McAuliffe turned southeast to Bastogne instead of continuing north along the road leading to Werbomont, which is some 25 miles north of Bastogne. He had decided to go to the VIII Corps headquarters and get briefed on the general situation. It was some time following his arrival at General Middleton's VIII Corps command post that he heard definitely for the first time that the 101st was to fight at Bastogne. General Gavin, who had left Werbomont late in the afternoon of the 18th to hand-carry the message to VIII Corps did not arrive until after dark. The delay caused General Middleton a considerable doubt; be had learned from higher authority that the 101st Division would fight at Bastogne but he did not know that the Division was his to use as he saw fit. General McAuliffe's party arrived at the VIII Corps command post, which was located in a former German barracks at the northwestern edge of Bastogne, at 1600 and from that time forward its members concerned themselves with getting ready to receive the Division. At that same moment Colonel Roberts, who had arrived ahead of his column, presented himself to General Middleton and reported that Combat Command B was on the road and would soon be in Bastogne.

Middleton asked Roberts, "How many teams can you make up?"

Roberts replied, "Three."

The General then said, "You will move without delay in three teams to these positions and counter enemy threats. One team will go to the southeast of Wardin, one team to the vicinity of Longvilly and one team to the vicinity of Noville. Move with the utmost speed. Hold these positions at all costs."

Roberts accepted the order without demur though at that moment he believed that the distribution of his force over so great an area would make it ineffective. But he made the mental reservation that the Corps commander must know the situation much better than he did himself. Middleton's decision was the initial tactical step which led finally to the saving of Bastogne." Combat Command B continued on its way moving north and east to carry out its orders.

The first two teams got through the town during daylight. The lead team, Team Cherry, under Lieutenant Colonel Henry T. Cherry, proceeded toward Longvilly, which was considered to be in the direction of the most immediate danger. The second team under Lieutenant Colonel James O'Hara headed toward the village of Wardin in the southeast. It was dark when the last team began moving through Bastogne. Its youthful commander, Major William R. Desobry, went to see Colonel Roberts with whom he had an especially close relationship. For a number of years Desobry had known the older man well; he was talking now to a man who was not only his commander but whom he regarded as a second father. Roberts pointed northward on the map to the village of Noville and told Desobry that he was to proceed there and hold the village. "It will be a close race to get there before the enemy," Roberts said. "You are young, and by tomorrow

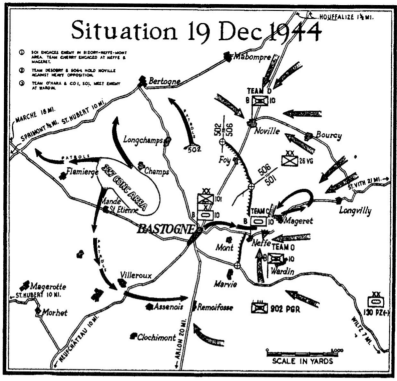

Map 2

morning you will probably be nervous. By midmorning the idea will probably come to you that it would be better to withdraw from Noville. When you begin thinking that, remember that I told you that it would be best not to withdraw until I order you to do so."

There were no maps at hand; one of Colonel Roberts' staff officers grabbed a Corps MP and sent him along with Desobry to put the team on the Noville road. A cavalry platoon leader from Desobry's column was sent on ahead to reconnoiter Noville, clear it if there were any enemy present, and then outpost it until the arrival of the main battle group. Desobry then dismounted one platoon of armored infantry, placed them on the backs of the three lead tanks and gave the word for the column to move north. Small groups of stragglers were already passing them, drifting southward. The column paid them no heed. The dark had already slowed the armor to a five-mile-per-hour pace and Desobry figured that he had no time to waste.

While McAuliffe and his party were on the road, at Mourmelon the Division was working on the problems of the move. The few hours before the Division began its march were utilized in preparations for departure and in partly providing those combat supplies which had been lost in Holland. Such things as mortars, rifle ammunition, entrenching tools, arctic overshoes, blankets and gas masks had fallen far below the normal and needed amounts in the tables of basic allowances. In the great emergency, Transportation Corps and Oise Base Section acted with utmost dispatch and rallied truck groups from Rouen and Paris. Many of the truckers had already been long on the road when they were ordered to Camp Mourmelon. They were intercepted, the trucks unloaded on the spot, and the drivers directed to their new destination. The first trucks arrived at 0900, December 18. The last of the 380 trucks needed for the movement of 11,000 men arrived at the camp at 1720 the same day. *[In the Strength Report for December 18, 1944, the Effective Strength of the 101st Division is listed as 805 officers and 11,035 enlisted men, a total of 11,840. The exact number who moved forward is not known as this total includes those not yet returned from pass and those who remained in Mourmelon to maintain the base camp.]* At 2000, eleven hours after the arrival of the first vehicles, the last man was out-loaded. As far as Bouillon, Belgium, the column ran with lights blazing. It was a calculated risk, taken by 101st for the sake of speed. The night was clear and the stars shone brightly. Had the Luftwaffe come on then, the story of Bastogne might have taken a different turn.

In Bastogne, General Middleton sketched the situation to General McAuliffe and Colonel Kinnard very roughly, telling them, "There has been a major penetration and certain of my units, especially the 106th and 28th Divisions, are broken." In the absence of the advance staff party Kinnard tried to function as a whole division staff during the conference. But after discussing matters with both the G-2 and G-3 sections at VIII Corps, he had only the vaguest picture of what was happening and felt altogether uncertain about both the friendly and enemy situations. He gathered that some of our armored elements - the 9th Armored Division and 10th Armored Division were mentioned - were out in front of Bastogne, but he could not pinpoint the spots where their roadblocks were. Because of their own uncertainty, both he and General McAuliffe became acutely concerned over plans for the night bivouac. Further than that, they worried that the column might be hit while it was still on the road or that it might even be caught by the German air while still a long way back.

While there was still light, they took a quick swing out over the area west of town and McAuliffe pointed out to Kinnard where he wanted the Division placed. It was a snap decision, yet it influenced the campaign importantly because it placed the Division in a sheltered forward assembly area until it was ready to strike. In the emergency Kinnard grabbed an MP private from the Corps and sent him to the crossroads at Sprimont to meet the division as it came on. He and General McAuliffe then went to the junction of the Arlon and Neufchateau roads in Bastogne to make another attempt to find the advance party. Colonel Kinnard had with him nine 1:100,000 and six 1:50,000 maps of the area. This was all that the Corps staff could give him with which to fight the operation ahead. When he returned from the reconnaissance, Kinnard searched at Corps headquarters for more maps but found that the map section was already moving out. From Corps he obtained an administrative order giving him the location of ammunition dumps, water points, evacuation hospitals and other installations.

However, despite Colonel Kinnard's best efforts, in the speed of the preparations to receive the Division, a good many points had not been securely pinned down. Trailing the last of the 82d

Division's column through Sprimont, Colonel T. L. Sherburne, acting commander of the 101st Division's artillery, and an assistant, Captain Cecil T. Wilson, arrived at the vital crossroads where one road leads off toward Bastogne and the other toward Bertogne at about 2000, December 18. Along the way leading north the rear elements of the 82d Division were blocking and stopping. Colonel Sherburne then wondered whether he couldn't get north and on to Werbomont more rapidly by veering from the Bertogne road and taking the long way through Bastogne. He asked an MP at the intersection whether any units of the 101st had gone that way; the MP wasn't certain about anything but referred him to an MP sergeant in a near-by house. The sergeant told him that General McAuliffe and his party had come along some hours before and had gone into Bastogne. So Colonel Sherburne returned to the man who was directing traffic and told him to turn all 101st Division parties toward Bastogne when they came to the intersection. He then continued on.

It appears likely that this small incident smoothed the whole path for the 101st Division. Two officers from the 502d Regiment, who were supposed to have gone with the advance party to Werbamont but had missed it, were re-routed by the MP a few minutes behind Sherburne to VIII Corps Headquarters.

They joined Kinnard and Starrett and drove west to Mande-St.-Étienne. Here they met a jeepload of 327th Infantry officers who had also missed the advance party. Kinnard now had enough personnel to set up the assembly area. An officer guide was posted on the Mande-St.Étienne road to direct the incoming column and Starrett went to work setting up a Division command post in a near-by farm house. The other officers reconnoitered their regimental areas and made their plans for the night dispositions. The hour was a little after 1800 on the 18th and there was not yet any sound of combat in the vicinity. A heavy maintenance company from 28th Division was already in Mande-St.Étienne. The company commander told Kinnard this was his area and he could not leave. Kinnard had to return to Bastogne to get an order from the corps commander to clear the area. Around General Middleton in the Corps command post there were now only six or eight officers.

From First Army, General Courtney Hodges, its commander, had called General Middleton and advised moving VIII Corps Headquarters to the rear. This had been done but General Middleton had stayed on in Bastogne with Colonel Stanton, his Deputy Chief of Staff, and several other members of his staff for the purpose, as he thought, of acquainting Major General Matthew B. Ridgway, the commander of XVIII Airborne Corps, with the situation, and of helping General McAuliffe get his situation in hand.

General Ridgway arrived at General Middleton's command post in Bastogne about 2030. He was still acting on the not wholly complete information which he had received from his several sources while at Camp Mourmelon. He understood that the 101st Division was to fight at Bastogne, but be thought that it was to operate under his Corps (the XVIII Airborne) though some 25 miles of distance intervened between the two airborne divisions. His acting corps commander, General Gavin, who had come and gone by this time, had brought the word to the 101st that it was to fight in the VIII Corps under General Middleton. But the situation still had not been clarified by higher authority. From Bastogne, General Ridgway called Headquarters First Army. It was at this time that the two Corps commanders got the new instructions which changed the problem of each and which at last set the lines along which the 82d and 101st Airborne Divisions, late of the SHAEF reserve, would operate in the Ardennes. Bastogne was to remain an VIII Corps problem and the 101st Division would operate under that Corps in that town. General Ridgway's XVIII Airborne Corps, less the 101st Division - so General Ridgway now learned for the first time - was to operate on the other side of the Bulge. On the strength of this new assignment, General Middleton subsequently called General Omar Bradley, Commanding General, 12th Army Group, and gave it as his estimate that the 101st Division and other troops assigned to defend Bastogne would probably be surrounded, since he had no reserve. General Bradley said that would be all right with him - to stand and defend even though it appeared probable that Bastogne would become encircled.

General McAuliffe decided to stay at Corps headquarters to get his mission for the next day. During the conference of the two corps commanders, Brigadier General Gerald J. Higgins, assistant division commander of the 101st, who had been called from England by General McAuliffe, arrived.

General Higgins and Colonel Kinnard went out to the Division assembly area. Lieutenant Starrett had found that the local schoolhouse was a better command post than the dwelling which Kinnard had designated and on his own initiative had made the change. He already had telephone lines strung to VIII Corps Headquarters and to the 501st Parachute Infantry area. An officer from the 506th Parachute Infantry who had missed the advance party reported at the command post and was given his sector.

In general, things were now looking a little more snug although one point of irritation had not been entirely eliminated. That was the captain commanding the heavy maintenance company who had refused to move his people out at Colonel Kinnard's request until Kinnard brought an order direct from General Middleton. General Higgins found him now completely blocking the highway over which 101st Division was coming in. His vehicles were parked three abreast and six or seven rows deep. It was an absolute impasse. General Higgins sought out the captain and made his protest. "I can't do anything about that," said the captain. "I have received an order from the General to move my vehicles out. I've made this block to make sure that none of my vehicles get by and get lost; it's the best way to collect them." Even after the situation was explained to him, he said he'd stay where be was. General Higgins then gave him a direct order to get his vehicles in single file along the road at once and himself set about urging the drivers over to the side of the highway.

This was but one incident in a night-long fight with the outgoing traffic. Every time the column of retreating vehicles came to a halt for a few minutes, some of the drivers fell asleep from exhaustion. When the road was again free for a few minutes and the forward vehicles got in motion, these sleeping drivers formed new traffic blocks back along the column. To keep things moving at all, it was necessary for officers and MPs to continue patrolling up and down the column, ready to rouse any slumberer who had tied things up.

That night in Bastogne was quiet, largely because the 28th Division was holding in place on commanding ground around Wiltz and fighting the enemy off for a few vital hours. Many stragglers were falling back through the town and the roads were jammed to the south and west but no attempt was made to hold any of these men at the time. VIII Corps was busy with its evacuation and Combat Command B of the 10th Armored Division and the 101st Division were engrossed in their own problems. Colonel Roberts, who had set up his command post in Hôtel Lebrun at 1800, December 18, found that it was difficult to persuade other units that were about to withdraw out of the Bastogne area even to give up their motor parks so that he could get his own vehicles off the streets.

The third major part of the Bastogne garrison, the 705th Tank Destroyer Battalion, under Lieutenant Colonel Clifford D. Templeton, got its marching orders at 1800 on December 18. It left Kohlscheid, Germany, at 2240, but could not proceed by the shortest route - Liège, Houffalize, Bastogne - because the enemy was already around Houffalize. The column of the 705th therefore moved by way of Laroche where it went into a defensive position along the heights six miles south of the town at 0915 on December 19. Colonel Templeton looked Laroche over and was thoroughly alarmed at what he found. American units were in confusion along the road. They were making little or no effort to adjust themselves to the situation or to set up a local defense. So in mid-morning Templeton sent two platoons with four tank destroyers to set up a roadblock to the north of the town. Leaving the battalion at Laroche, he then went on to Neufchâteau, where VIII Corps Headquarters was newly established. There General Middleton told him to get on into Bastogne and attach his outfit to the 101st Division. An officer was sent back to Laroche to bring the battalion on but to leave the roadblock force in place.

Colonel Templeton and his command section, after reporting to General McAuliffe, started northwest to meet the oncoming column. At Bertogne the section was ambushed by a German party armed with two machine guns, one self-propelled gun and several small antiaircraft guns. The opening fire wounded three men, destroyed a jeep and forced the abandonment of the armored command vehicle. Templeton's men withdrew along the road for about half a mile with all their weapons engaging the enemy. This action took place about 1500 on the 19th and was over in twenty minutes.

Templeton radioed to his battalion to expect the German roadblock at Bertogne. He then told them, however, that the roadblock could be overwhelmed and the battalion was to "come any way possible to Bastogne, but get there." He did not know that the Bastogne road was impassable because the bridge above the town was out. In the late afternoon the command section returned to Bastogne to establish its command post. Templeton then radioed the commander of the supply train to "find a haven in the west and hook up with some big friends." He felt quite certain that his train would get through safely because the one M18 accompanying it was capable of dealing with any roving enemy tank or infantry group along the way. Colonel Templeton's 705th Tank Destroyer Battalion reached Bastogne at 2030, December 19, by the route Laroche-Champlon-Bastogne.

With the arrival of the 705th Tank Destroyer Battalion, all the major elements which would be present in Bastogne during the siege (the first phase of the defense of the town) were gathered. The 101st Division and Combat Command B had begun the fight that morning and the tank destroyers were now ready to link their power with that of the armor and the infantry. Men of every unit had morale of the highest quality and with their weapons each was capable of stiffening the other. It was a matter of finding the way through courage, resource, and good will.

3. TEAM CHERRY

O N THE EVENING of December 18, Roberts ordered Team Cherry of his Combat Command B to move out along the road leading east and go into position near Longvilly. It thereby became the first of the Bastogne reinforcements to move out and engage the enemy. The force under command of Lieutenant Colonel Henry T. Cherry (Commanding Officer, 3d Tank Battalion, 10th Armored Division) included the 3d Tank Battalion, Company C of the 20th Armored Infantry Battalion, the 3d Platoon of Company C of the 55th Engineer Battalion and the 2d Platoon of Troop B of the 90th Cavalry Squadron. *[All the material from which this narrative is produced is based on the interview with the members of Team Cherry. The records of Team Cherry were completely destroyed during the Christmas Eve bombings of Bastogne and consequently there is no official record of the operation of Colonel Cherry's force other than the interview and what Colonel Roberts, commanding officer, Combat Command B, 10th Armored Division, could say of Team Cherry's operation.]*

They went on into the darkness, knowing only this of their situation, that some parts of Combat Command Reserve of the 9th Armored Division were supposed to be in the vicinity of Longvilly and that the enemy was reported advancing toward that town from the east. Their march was uneventful. First Lieutenant Edward P. Hyduke (Commanding Officer, Company A, 3d Tank Battalion), who had the advance guard, came to a halt just short of Longvilly at 1920. The town is on low ground and its streets seemed to be already jammed with the vehicles of Combat Command Reserve. Leaving the main body, Colonel Cherry went forward to the command post of Combat Command

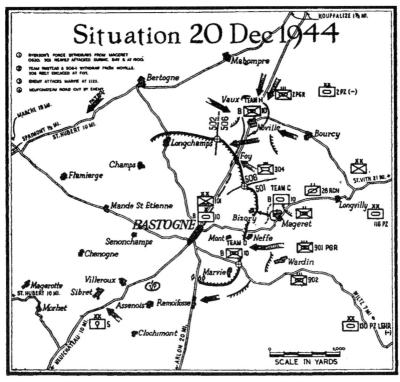

Map 3

Reserve to learn their intentions. But they had no plan and did not know whether they would stay or get out. So Cherry returned to his force, which was then refueling on the road, and told Hyduke to make a reconnaissance and occupy ground west of Longvilly before dawn came. The main body was to stay one thousand yards west of the town until there was a change in the situation of the Combat Command Reserve. At 2300 on the 18th Cherry returned to headquarters in Bastogne to tell Colonel Roberts how things were going. As he went through Magéret he noticed that Combat Command Reserves trains were headed for the rear. Roberts told him that he was to cover the main body of the Combat Command Reserve if it withdrew, but in any case he was to hold at Longvilly.

The road was already plagued with stragglers, most of them moving in trucks and half-tracks back toward Bastogne. They knew nothing except they had last seen the enemy about six miles east of Longvilly along the main road. Men asked what the Germans had, they repeated: "Tanks, tanks, tanks," and then moved on to the rear.

Combat Command Reserve set up roadblocks to the north and east of Longvilly, with one battalion of infantry and another of tanks supporting the blocks, and two batteries of artillery helping to cover them from a position next to the town. But there was no close-in defense around the houses. Looking these dispositions over, Lieutenant Hyduke decided there was danger that the enemy might come in from the south. So he sent his platoon of cavalry in that direction with instructions to withdraw quickly if the pressure became heavy. Seven light tanks were placed forward with four medium tanks to the right covering them. Infantry units formed an outpost north of the position. One of the field artillery batteries from Combat Command Reserve tied in with Lieutenant Hyduke's party and shortly thereafter opened fire to the eastward, though Hyduke never learned what they were firing at.

At 2340, Combat Command Reserve, 9th Armored Division, began its withdrawal from Longvilly, though it was not until two hours later, while Colonel Cherry was returning to his team, that he got word by radio from Hyduke that Team Cherry was now holding alone.

The next few minutes brought some more distressing news to the commander. In Neffe he met a wounded enlisted man who said that his vehicle had been shot up near Magéret. Then a sergeant told him that a strong German patrol had entered Magéret just after midnight. This meant that the Germans were across the road between Cherry and his Team. Cherry radioed Captain William F. Ryerson (Commanding Officer of Company C, 20th Armored Infantry Battalion, 10th Armored Division), who had been left in command at Longvilly, to get a patrol to Magéret and reopen the road. Two squads of infantry were sent in a half-track on this mission. They dismounted before reaching the village and approached it stealthily. Within a few minutes they had located three enemy tanks and an infantry force which they guessed to be about one company, in positions around the crossroads at Magéret. They had come in along the one side of the town that was not being covered by an enemy tank, and while they waited there they heard another armored vehicle coming up behind them. For a few seconds they were in a cold sweat, thinking they were about to be trapped by a fourth tank. Instead, it proved to be an American tank destroyer. The infantrymen and the tank destroyer crew discussed their chances and decided they weren't strong enough to attack Magéret. So they returned to Ryerson. By then Captain Ryerson had heard from Colonel Roberts that he was to commandeer any American men or equipment which he could use. So he drafted the tank destroyer into his outfit.

The discovery that the enemy was across the Combat Team's rear, quickly followed by Ryerson's report of the enemy strength which his patrol had found at Magéret, convinced Colonels Roberts and Cherry that the situation was now such that Longvilly could not be held. Colonel Cherry ordered the advance guard under Lieutenant Hyduke to hold its ground at Longvilly while the main body tried to beat its way back through Magéret. These orders, which arrived at 0830, December 19, turned the advance guard into a rear guard. Colonel Cherry went back to his command post which was in a stoutly walled château three hundred yards south of Neffe, and stayed there awaiting developments. The command post force, the rear guard and the main body were each engaged during the entire day in widely separated actions.

By daybreak of the 19th Hyduke was set up on three sides of Longvilly and ready to defend the rear. However, the closing of the road at Magéret by the Germans had kept many of Combat Command Reserve's vehicles from withdrawing, and after taking to the road, they sat there, blocking all traffic. There was a heavy nebelwerfer shelling of Hyduke's lines in the early morning and the area then quieted until 1000. The position was reasonably safe from frontal assault for the ground to the north of the main road was marshy for ten yards and facing toward the marsh was an embankment much too steep for tanks to cross. On the right of the road the ground fell away too sharply for tanks. A large culvert a short distance ahead of the position was set for demolition.

The morning engagement opened with the sighting of two enemy tanks about 1500 yards southeast of Longvilly but the visibility was so poor because of fog that only the vague outlines of the tanks could be seen. A shot from the Germans hit a tank in the Combat Command Reserve group along the road, locking the turret. All of the American armor returned the fire and both enemy tanks went up in flames. After this there was a prolonged shelling of Longvilly.

At 1400 the enemy armor put direct fire on Lieutenant Hyduke's position from front and left flank, disabling two half-tracks and one light tank at the tail of the column. Five minutes later the enemy knocked out two more medium tanks 150 yards in front of the burning half-track. An enemy antitank gun on the enemy's right hit a Combat Command Reserve tank which had remained in position with the lone artillery battery. The battery then promptly took off.

The groups on the road were now almost in a state of panic and when some of the vehicles tried to swing around the column, the road became more jammed than ever. One group of stragglers which had been organized to cover the left flank fled their position, leaving that part of the ground to only 23 infantrymen of Company C, 20th Armored Infantry Battalion.

Lieutenant Hyduke had been given authority to take over any portion of Combat Command Reserve which withdrew but he found that it was impossible to do so. However, despite the panicky state of the stragglers he was able to maintain close control of his own force and continued to engage the enemy until 1430 when Colonel Cherry ordered him to fall back on Captain Ryerson's force.

But that order couldn't be carried out. The road was absolutely blocked. Moreover, he couldn't order his men out of their vehicles because enemy foot troops were now moving in on his flanks and the whole area was under heavy bullet fire. Some of the tanks turned around on the road and tried to get back to the ground they had defended.

In this period of threshing around, five of his seven light tanks and one tankdozer and a tank recovery vehicle were destroyed. The half-tracks at the front of the column had to be abandoned and soon after the men got out of them, two more medium tanks were hit by artillery fire. One medium tank got cut off and when last seen was trying to fight off an attack by German infantry. The last medium tank received a direct hit on its track as it tried to get out. The three remaining light tanks, including one that had belonged to an artillery forward observer, were destroyed by their crews to prevent capture. By 1500 most of the survivors had escaped the scene of all this wreckage and joined Captain Ryerson.

Ryerson had had a tough time carrying out his mission because of the traffic jam along the road, but by 0945, December 19, his column had reached a point 300 yards east of Magéret. As his lead tank came round the last bend in the road a shell from an enemy antitank gun in Magéret hit it frontally, burning up the tank and killing or injuring all members of the crew. The road ran through a cut at this point and the burning tank plugged it completely. The stalled column then became a general target for intense shelling and small-arms fire from the German armor and infantry force in the village.

Captain Ryerson's infantry then dismounted from their vehicles and moved forward to reconnoiter the enemy position.

The high ground on both sides of the burning tank protected them for a little way but they could not go on past the ridge because the down-slope was getting heavy bullet and mortar fire. Two 105mm. assault guns maneuvered up to the ridge and shelled a tree line where they thought the German infantry was holding. The small-arms fire from the village soon slacked off a bit.

From the rear, two antiaircraft half-tracks from the 9th Armored Division came on past Captain Ryerson's force, moving toward Bastogne. Ryerson's men tried to stop them but they drove on heedlessly until they turned the curve and saw the burning tank. The crews then jumped for safety without trying to save their vehicles. The Germans shelled both vehicles and now they blocked the road doubly.

Next the gun crews along the ridge saw an American command car and a Sherman tank, complete with cerise panels, whip out of Magéret and move north. They were quite startled for a moment and held their fire. By the time they had decided these vehicles were being used by the enemy, it was too late to do anything; they had moved out of range.

Two batteries of the 73d Armored Field Artillery came up behind the column and on finding the road blocked moved out north and west and going by way of Bizory got into the line of the main American position (the 501st's lines).

By about 1500 the fire from Magéret had subsided so appreciably that a force composed of 18 infantrymen, two medium tanks and a 105mm. assault gun were sent against the village, moving through the fields on the right flank. One of the Shermans got hung up on an embankment and drew a great deal of fire but was able to return to the column. The rest of the force worked its way into the northeast part of the village, receiving some shellfire from the southeast of the village as they went. At the main crossroads they could see a roadblock with one German tank and an American M4. This armor did not move or fire and the party concluded that it was already destroyed. In the southern part of the village they could see two more German tanks, an American half-track, a jeep and a German ambulance. The heavy guns with the party could not find a position from which to fire and the infantry could do nothing effective.

From the rear of his column Captain Ryerson was called by his antitank officer, 2d Lieutenant Early B. Gilligan, who told him that twenty half-tracks loaded with men forward dismounted and send along any tanks that he might see. The new men consisted of about 200 stragglers from different units who had retreated into the Bastogne area from other actions. They were mostly tankers. Lieutenant Gilligan got them out of the half-tracks, but only forty of them, with three captains and two lieutenants from Combat Command Reserve and a few officers from Hyduke's section, moved up toward the fire fight. The others fled across the fields to the north.

"The forty men who stuck were organized into four squads and at 1600, December 19, this force moved against the southeast part of the village, supported by a section of medium tanks. But the tanks could not get over the ground that lay south of the road and the men were not inclined to go far ahead of the tanks.

Within the village several of the German vehicles which had been to the south stated to move north toward the maw crossing. To the amazement of Ryerson's men, the German tank forming the roadblock, which they had thought to be dead all the time, suddenly started up and moved out of the way. Captain Ryerson's force had been for hours within plain view of this tank at a range of 600 yards without receiving any attention from it. The American tank now put it under fire at once and set the German tank ablaze.

There was still so much shelling from the south of the village however, that the American guns had to stay immobile and the small force of infantry could not get forward. Prisoners they had taken said that the enemy infantry group comprised about 120 men. The 40-man force which had attacked toward the south of Magéret had no communication with Captain Ryerson's main force and later that evening somewhat less than half of them came back. They bad made no real progress.

Since noon Captain Ryerson had been aware that infantry forces were coming to his aid from Bastogne. He didn't know which units were coming but the expectation of relief encouraged his efforts to take Magéret.

Through its various misadventures, Team Cherry as a whole had come to a pass where it could no longer confront the oncoming enemy and where most of its energies would be directed to saving its remaining elements, and covering its own flanks and rear. Whether the German advance into Bastogne from the eastward could be checked and thrown into recoil now depended on the forces of the 101st Division itself.

4. FIRST MEETING WITH THE ENEMY

A T BASTOGNE, THE 101st Division played in luck from the beginning and the luck began weeks before the siege started. In the early part of November a young lieutenant colonel, Julian Ewell, commanding the 501st Parachute Infantry on the Neder Rijn front in Holland, took a busman's holiday and spent two days of his leave at Bastogne. *[Colonel Ewell told Colonel Marshall about this during their conversation. The two men had a close acquaintanceship extending back to the Normandy campaign. However, Colonel Ewell was rated this way by all of his fellows. He mentioned his visit to Bastogne as a matter only of passing interest. It seems likely that this remarkable coincidence would never have been brought to light except that Ewell had to explain how he knew his own troops were on the wrong road initially. Colonel Ewell was badly wounded a few hours after the interview.]*

It was the luck of war that in giving the march order before leaving Camp Mourmelon, General McAuliffe had put the 501st Parachute Infantry at the head of the column. *[The order of march directed by General McAuliffe was: 501st, 506th, 502d, 327th, with 81st Antiaircraft Battalion following the 501st and 326th Engineers following the 506th.]* It was the luck of war again that Ewell got away well in advance of the column on December 18 and was the first commander to arrive in the vicinity of the bivouac. He ran into a wire-stringing detail there, asked what they were doing, found that they were men from the 101st Division and then followed the wires into the Division command post. Then he got ready to guide his own men in.

All down the route over which he had come Colonel Ewell

had found the traffic blocking and stopping, and he didn't expect his 501st to come up to him before 2300 because of this congestion. But it beat that schedule by half an hour and Ewell's unit was closed into its area by 2400. General McAuliffe knew at midnight that by then he had one regiment ready.

Lieutenant Colonel (now Colonel) Julian J. Ewell, Commanding Officer, 501st Parachute Infantry

Bastogne looking north

Bastogne looking south

Earlier in the night (December 18) Ewell had talked to Generals McAuliffe and Higgins. The one thing on which all three commanders agreed was that no one could be sure of anything. Ewell said of himself that he was as much in the dark as any man present. But he told his commander, General McAuliffe, that he thought he should be given a definite assignment. It was a big request, the situation considered.

The main street of Bastogne from the monastery command post of the 501st Parachute Infantry. The cold and snow made movement difficult and living uncomfortable.

McAuliffe and Middleton conferred on it.

The commander's index finger pointed out along the road running eastward - toward the ridges where Ewell had walked in November - although neither General Middleton nor General McAuliffe ever knew that he had seen the ground.7 The enemy was coming that way. At Corps headquarters the 9th Armored Division was thought to have a roadblock somewhere around Longvilly and the 10th Armored Division a block farther west toward Neffe. The 9th's block was thought to be surrounded; the 10th's block was supposed to be engaged but not yet surrounded. *[This was the situation as Colonel Kinnard understood it to be and as he made note of it at the time. But it was not precisely the situation as it existed.]*

General Middleton had described the situation at these blocks when General McAuliffe had reported to him, and he had said: "There is a battle now going on for Bastogne." He spoke of the block out along the Longvilly road as "surrounded" and indicated the positions of the three blocks which Combat Command B of the 10th Armored was maintaining to the east, northeast and southeast of the city. *[The discrepancy between this and the preceding paragraph is a difference in Kinnard's and McAuliffe's understanding of the situation of the roadblocks. In any case it is inconsequential.]* The Corps commander had no specific plan for the employment of the 101st Division. The news that he was to have that division had come so recently that he had had no time to prepare a plan. At first General McAuliffe could think of nothing. At 2200 he suggested to General Middleton that a combat team be sent east to develop the situation. That idea appealed to General McAuliffe simply as a "good old Leavenworth solution of the problem." It was wholly consistent with General Middleton's concern for the preservation of the other elements of his command. As General Middleton reasoned the problem, so long as the 10th Armored team was already employed in the east, it was not urgent that the 101st

Bomb damage in Bastogne

Airborne Division develop the situation there, although it was sound practice to reinforce the armored team's roadblock, since it was becoming evident that the weight of the enemy attack was coming down the Longvilly road.

Middleton and McAuliffe sent for Ewell. He had been spending a part of his time unprofitably at the road intersections trying to get information from men who were straggling in from the north and northeast. All talked vaguely and dispiritedly. Man after man said to him: "We have been wiped out," and then stumbled away through the dark. They did not know where they had been. They had no idea where they were going. Colonel Ewell and his officers tried several times to draw these men out, then gave them up as a bad job and paid no further attention. Ewell reached his separate conclusion that any quest for information concerning the enemy, other than going out bodily after it, was useless.

The exact mission given Ewell was to "seize the road junction at 676614 and hold it." That would put him out the eastern road well beyond Longvilly. Middleton told him that combat Command Reserve of the 9th Armored Division had a roadblock At that point which was supposed to be "isolated" and that the 110th Infantry was supposedly still maintaining a command post at Allerborn. From the assembly area of the 501st Parachute Infantry, it was nine and a half miles to the road junction. However, that distant point did not enter into General McAuliffe's instructions to Ewell or into Ewell's estimate of what the 501st would be able to accomplish. McAuliffe was not sure where the enemy would crowd him first, but he thought it most likely that they would roll on him from the east. That bad as much to do with his assignment of Ewell as did the fact that the armored roadblocks were involved with the enemy.

Then General McAuliffe simply pointed to the map and moved his finger along in the direction of Longvilly. He said: "Ewell, move out along this road at six o'clock, make contact, attack and clear up the situation."

Ewell didn't ask a question. He said: "Yes, Sir," saluted and went on his way."

Recalling that scene some days afterward, General McAuliffe was to remark: "There were many men and commanders in my operation who did outstanding things. But Ewell's was the greatest gamble of all. It was dark. He had no knowledge of the enemy. I could not tell him what he was likely to meet. But he has a fine eye for ground and no man has more courage. He was the right man for the spot I put him in."

Of the few maps which the 101st Division had obtained from VIII Corps headquarters, twenty went with Ewell's combat team as it started to march. It wasn't enough to go around. Lieutenant Colonel Clarence F. Nelson, commanding the 907th Glider Field Artillery Battalion, had only one map scaled 1:100,000 from which to provide his firing data. So as the movement got under way, he had sketches drawn up for the forward observers. On the sketches all control points and critical features-such as crossroads, bridges, woods and towns-were marked and numbered. The observers knew the locations of the batteries. In this way the artillery operation was co-ordinated.

The offensive mission was limited to the one combat team, Ewell's. McAuliffe bad decided right at the beginning that a

The underground message center of the 101st Airborne Division in Bastogne.

Vehicle in Bastogne camouflaged with sheets from village homes.

successful defense of Bastogne depended on the utmost harboring of his reserves at every stage of operation, and having sent Ewell forth, he decided to sit on Bastogne with the rest of his Division until something new developed.

That same idea - conservation of force - guided Colonel Ewell in his opening moves. In giving his battalion commanders the march order, he told Major Raymond V. Bottomly, Jr., who was leading out with the 1st Battalion of the 501st, that he was not to put out flank security until he reached Magéret; otherwise, the progress of the column would be much too slow. But in line with the governing principle he added the instruction to all commanders that if they met opposition, they were to "take it slow and easy." Being familiar with his men and their methods in past campaigns, he knew that they tended to throw themselves directly on the target. These methods had worked in Normandy and Holland. But from what he had seen of the Bastogne terrain in November, he had concluded that his main chance lay in "fire

A column of men marching in the vicinity of Bastogne. The rolling ground and pine forest are typical of the area.

and maneuver" rather than in shock action. He felt that his whole operation should be guided by this principle. He said to them; "I don't want you to try to beat the enemy to death."

The regiment took off at 0600, December 19, passing its command post on the minute.26 Battery B of the 81st Airborne Antiaircraft Battalion - seven 57mm. guns - moved out behind 1st Battalion. The 101st Airborne Division's Reconnaissance Troop, which bad been attached to Ewell's 501st Parachute Infantry, started through the town ahead of Major Bottomly's men. The observers and the liaison party from the artillery moved out with the lead infantry company. The artillery battalion stayed in the bivouac area two miles west of Bastogne waiting for the infantry to find the enemy.

Ewell went forward at 0700. The light was just beginning to break. Already, he felt vaguely familiar with the terrain and the first thing that happened strengthened his confidence in his memory. At the first intersection past the town, he found the 1st Battalion moving down the wrong road - toward Marvie. He saw from memory of the ground, without looking at the map, that they were going the wrong way. He recalled them and got them pointed toward Longvilly. The Reconnaissance Platoon, having proceeded farthest along the wrong road, thus got behind the battalion column, and raced to catch up.

Ewell's column passed on down the road that follows the line of the creek toward Neffe. To their left the hills rose evenly from the edge of the right-of-way-fairly easy slopes up which an infantryman might run without undue exertion. Ahead, they could see very little. The road dipped and turned around the hill facings of the little valley and the morning fog lay so thick that the visibility toward the south, where the land opens up beyond the line of the creek, was limited to 500 yards.

The 1st Battalion had been on the march for a little more than two hours, and the advance party was being passed through by the Reconnaissance Platoon, when the column was fired on by

The village of Neffe. Early in the morning of December 19 the enemy captured this crossroads village. During that day the position was held against the 501st Parachute Infantry. The Neffe Chateau is int he clump of trees on the right; the road to the left leads to Bastogne.

a machine gun from along the road and just westward of Neffe. The first burst of fire did no damage but the battalion hit the dirt. They had need to, for they were looking straight down the groove toward the enemy position; for the last 700 yards the road runs straight and almost level into Neffe. To right of the road, the ground fell off sharply to the creek. To the left were the gently sloping hills, and Bottomly deployed his men that way. Ewell told him to go ahead and develop his situation. Shells began whipping along the road and Bottomly sent word back to Ewell that he thought he was being opposed by two tanks and two platoons of infantry.

Colonel Ewell took himself off, leaving Bottomly to direct his own fight. He had already tasted the shellfire and he didn't want to tempt it, unnecessarily. Back beyond the road's first turning, about 100 yards from Bottomly's skirmish line, there

Neffe, scene of heavy fighting by the 501st Parachute Infantry and Team Cherry, after it was recaptured.

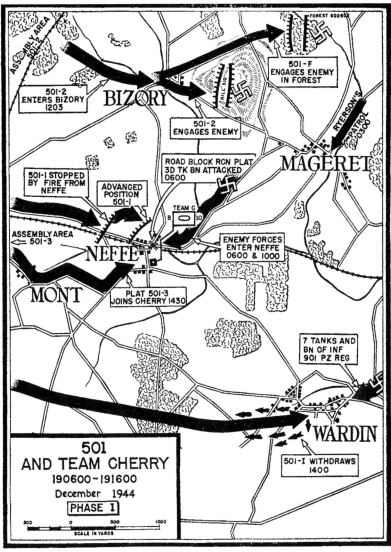

Map 4

was a pocket in the hillside to left of the road where a stone house fitted snugly. There Colonel Ewell set up his command post.

It soon became clear to him that his 1st Battalion would not be able to overcome the roadblock because of the German tanks. The tanks were firing from a defilade close into the hillside where the road runs down to Neffe from Bizory. Bottomly couldn't bring the 57mms. to bear because the Neffe-Bastogne road ran so straight for the last half mile. About 1000, convinced that his 1st Battalion was stopped, Ewell decided to bring the rest of his regiment out of Bastogne. But this was easier said than done.

The VIII Corps was rushing the evacuation of its last units and their troops were streaming through town across the line of march the rest of the 501st Parachute Infantry would have to take. The 2d Battalion fought its way through this traffic during the next hour and Colonel Ewell ordered them on to an assembly area on the reverse of the gently sloping ridge north of Major Bottomly's position. He figured that he would put them out to the left, closed up so that they could be deployed at the most advantageous moment.

Lieutenant Colonel Nelson, commanding officer of the 907th Glider Field Artillery Battalion, and Captain Gerald J. McGlone, commanding officer of Battery B, 907th, had gone forward to Colonel Ewell the minute the radio flashed word that the 1st Battalion of the 501st had met fire at Neffe. McGlone got his battery into position 500 yards northeast of Bastogne on the left of the Longvilly road, and opened fire as soon as he was in position, which was only a few minutes after 1000, December 19. The fog was still thick and the battery was working under several other handicaps - its radios had never been tested and five of its guns had never been fired. But they spoke now from a distance of only 1,000 yards behind Bottomly's skirmish line. Having weighed the risk that the enemy might flow on around Ewell's narrow front - and accepted it - Nelson decided that one battery was enough in that particular position. He put Battery A, under Captain Lowell B. Bigelow, into the action from a position near the battalion command post, 1,000 yards west of Bastogne. Luck rode with him. The defilade where he had placed Battery B on the spur of the moment was so well chosen that the guns were to work there for almost a month without receiving a single round of German counter-battery fire.

This day, however, the batteries had no need to worry about anything coming in on them. The only heavy support for the German attack was from their tanks and it was all close-up fire directed against Ewell's infantry units. The American artillery fire was turned mainly against the tanks and the small groups of German infantry. There were many such targets.

Colonel Ewell sized up his situation. In 1st Battalion, Companies B and C were in skirmish line, while Company A was collected in reserve. Major Bottomly had deployed most of his strength to the north of the highway but he had managed to find room for one platoon in the ground south of the creek and rail line. The battalion had put two mortars into operation almost immediately and their fire was shaking down the houses around the enemy roadblock in Neffe.

But an attempt to get the 1st Battalion's left flank forward had failed. From Neffe, the north road climbs gradually through a shallow draw to the small farming community of Bizory. The country hereabouts is all uninterrupted grazing land except for the small but thick tree plantations and clusters of farmhouses

A 105mm M3 howitzer being fired by members of the 907th Glider Field Artillery Battalion during the siege of Bastogne.

which appear as villages on the map. The dominant terrain features are the long and quite regular ridges which run generally in a north-south line. These hills are gently undulating and the hillsides are quite smooth. From the tops of the commanding ridges one can see great distances on a clear day. The reverse slopes of the hills are smooth and are usually accessible from either end of the hills, making them highly useful to artillery and armor. The roads are close enough together so that vehicles can move to the ridges from either direction. When the country is covered with snow, nothing obtrudes on the landscape except the small black patches of forest. The ridges fall away in gently sloping draws which provide clear fields of fire to the flank and make it easily possible to cover the main lines of communication. The road from Neffe to Bizory rises gradually for a distance, providing a perfect slot for fire from the low ground around Neffe. Bottomly had made one pass in this direction and shells from the enemy armor had fairly blistered the little valley.

Ewell decided that as long as the enemy tanks were in Neffe, his 1st Battalion couldn't move in any direction. He ordered the 2d Battalion to seize Bizory. That hamlet is in the same draw up which the tanks had shot at Bottomly's men, but the ground flattens out at Bizory so that the place can't be seen from Neffe. This detail, however, Ewell couldn't see from the rear, but he was curious to find out about it. The map told him that the ridge adjacent to Bizory was the high ground and would be of use to him. He wanted to see if the enemy force east of there was holding a continuous position and he sent his 2d Battalion forward to find out.

His decision, so casually made, probably contributed as much to the salvation of Bastogne as anything that happened during the first few critical days. Colonel Ewell was still strongly of the opinion that he was being opposed by only a minor roadblock. But when he determined to extend the 501st and sweep forward, he made it a certainty that the oncoming Germans would suddenly collide with Americans who were attacking along a broad front. This was the thing the Germans least expected. Until it happened they had been meeting small or disorganized units, which they quickly encircled and overcame.

The shock of the discovery threw them off stride. They recoiled, hesitated and lost priceless, unreclaimable hours and opportunity because of their own confusion. In that action, a few American platoons hardened the fate of armies. But Ewell thought of none of these things as he ordered his 2d Battalion, 501st Parachute Infantry, to seize Bizory. He reflected on them later in his command post in the Bastogne monastery which the German artillery had made one of the best-ventilated buildings in all of Belgium. *[On the day of the interview the building was hit and shelled repeatedly. In the Nunnery yards that morning a truck loaded with 200 mines was blown up. Not one particle of the bodies of the 12 men who were loading it could be found. Whether the truck had been hit by a shell was never determined.]*

5. EAST OF BASTOGNE

THE THIRD BATTALION of the 501st Parachute Infantry had been caught in the traffic snarl west of Bastogne and was at a standstill. Colonel Ewell checked on them at 1200, December 19, and found that they had scarcely moved at all. After trying to get out of town, the battalion had backtracked, only to find that other routes were likewise clogged with outgoing troops. Yet even this delay had its benefits. Some of the infantrymen lacked helmets, rifles and ammunition. They begged them from the armored troops of Combat Command B, 10th Armored Division, who were in the town, and thus in the interval the battalion became somewhat better equipped. Colonel Ewell ordered Lieutenant Colonel George M. Griswold, commanding the 3d Battalion, to march his battalion to Mont, a little hamlet lying south of the Neffe road.

It seemed like the best opportunity to get the battalion out of Bastogne. Ewell also directed that one of Griswold's companies

The Bastogne road entering the outskirts of Mont.

be sent down the Wiltz road to cover the 3d Battalion's right flank as it moved. Colonel Griswold was told to send the company to the bend in the road directly east of the village of Marvie. Colonel Ewell planned to send the 3d Battalion against Neffe from the southwest after it had reached Mont, but he issued no orders to the effect at the time. He followed his usual plan of giving his subordinate commanders only a limited objective.

At 1203 the 2d Battalion took Bizory without opposition except for unobserved fire from the German tanks in Neffe. Still convinced that the Neffe roadblock was the only immediate threat to his front, Ewell ordered his 2d Battalion to advance and seize Magéret. By this move he figured he would box the tanks in so that he could then move against them either from front or rear according to the advantages of the ground. But he specified that Major Sammie N. Homan, commander of the 2d Battalion, send one of his companies to seize the patch of woods directly north of Magéret. This wood is a small plantation of very tall spruces. Ewell saw that the long ridge running across to the spruces dominated Magéret in the valley. It seemed to him that putting one company there might cover the approach to Magéret. *[Ewell did not know what had been happening to Team Cherry around Magéret.]*

Major Homan started out by road from Bizory to Magéret, but his route march ended quickly. At the crest of Hill 510 he ran into German infantry in dug-in positions: they were the Reconnaissance Platoon of the 26th Volksgrenadier Division. Homan took this first jolt almost without loss; not so, the enemy. Their line was moving forward from the foxholes and coming over the hill when the 2d Battalion mortars and Nelson's artillery caught them with full blast. The paratroopers saw a number of the enemy fall before the survivors ran back. Deploying the rest of his battalion, Homan sent Company F to the left to seize the coveted wood. When this extension was completed he reported to Colonel Ewell by radio that his hands were full and he was now engaged along his entire front. "For the time being," he said, "I cannot think of taking Magéret."

Colonel Griswold's 3d Battalion reached Mont and found one of the engineer roadblocks outposting that point, but the further operation of the main body of the battalion was compromised by the nature of the ground between Mont and Neffe. The two villages are little more than a mile apart and from Neffe one can look right down the little valley and see Mont clearly. The tanks of Panzer Lehr, which were at Neffe, were shipping a few shells toward Griswold's infantry. It seemed possible that a small party might work its way toward Neffe but the ground was much too naked for the exposure of any large force. Colonel Griswold stopped his 3d Battalion where it was.

Company L which had drawn the assignment on the extreme right flank, was instructed to prowl the three large woods west and northwest of the village of Wardin. At 1330 Company I reported that they had checked the three woods and found no enemy. Colonel Ewell then told Company I to advance to Wardin and make contact with a friendly armored roadblock that was supposed to be there. Ewell had not been told officially of the existence of this force but had heard of it quite casually from someone walking down the road. *[Ewell said he had no prior knowledge of this group. Yet Kinnard and McAuliffe had received the information from Middleton.]*

The company went on to make the contact Ewell had ordered. But for all practical effect, the stranger who had mentioned that there was a friendly roadblock near by might just as well have left his words unsaid.

This was Team O'Hara of Combat Command B, 10th Armored Division, which on the night of December 18 had taken up position on the high ground south of Wardin just short of the woods. The night had been quiet except for the stragglers coming through - mostly rear echelon people from the 28th Division

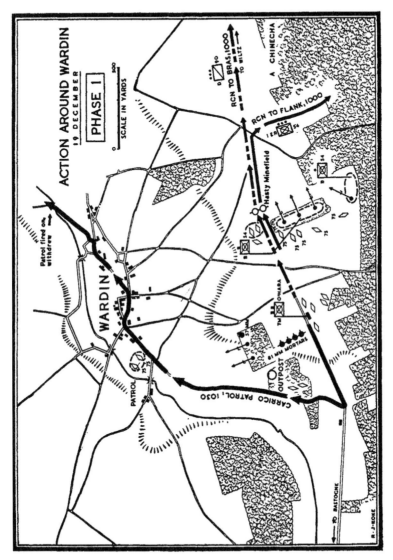

Map 5

whose idea of the enemy situation was confused. The morning of December 19 opened with fog. About 1000 the trickle of stragglers stopped altogether. This worried Team O'Hara for they figured it must mean that the enemy was coming next. They put out a platoon as a reconnaissance screen to the east which moved slowly along the road to Bras. At 1140 they engaged and destroyed a Volkswagen on the Wiltz-Bastogne highway. Just as they opened fire they saw the head of the enemy column break through the fog a few hundred yards away - two Mark IV tanks and a personnel carrier. The platoon had nothing with which to fight armor and so it cleared out rapidly, reporting its findings by radio. As a result of the message, unobserved fire was put on Bras by the 420th Armored Field Artillery Battalion.

At about the same time Captain Edward A. Carrigo, Team S-2, and First Lieutenant John D. Devereaux, commanding Company B of the 54th Armored Infantry Battalion, were entering Wardin from the southwest and finding it unhealthy The town was wrapped in fog; they could scarcely see anything at fifty yards' range. But they prowled on through the town and just as they got beyond it a projectile of antitank size hit the front bumper of their jeep. Nothing was hurt, but the two officers increased their speed and reported that there were people moving into Wardin who were quite unfriendly.

By noon of the 19th the visibility lengthened to 800 yards. Second Lieutenant Theodore R. Hamer, observer for the 420th Armored Field Artillery Battalion, moved forward to the top of a small hill. There were five tanks of Team O'Hara on the crest when he got there. But before he had a chance to observe for fire, his own tank was hit twice from the left by a high-velocity gun, wounding Hamer and three other crew members. One man was incinerated inside the tank. Another medium tank was bit in the turret by a shell that killed the gunner. The driver backed the tank down the hill wildly, not stopping until his vehicle became bogged; the tank could not be salvaged and later bad to be

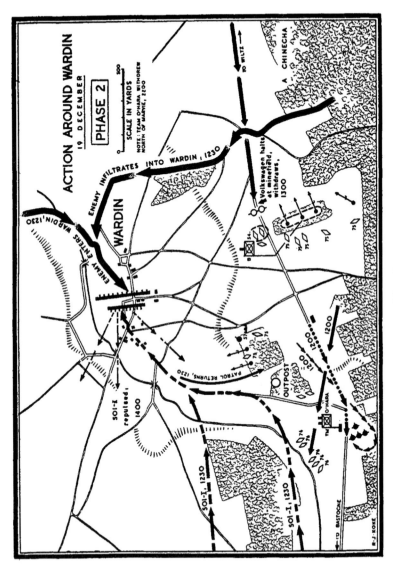

ACTION AROUND WARDIN
19 DECEMBER
PHASE 2

SCALE IN YARDS
0   500
NOTE: TEAM O'HARA, WITHDREW
NORTH OF MARVIE, 2100

TO WILTZ

A CHINECHA

Volkswagen halts
at minefield,
withdraws,
1300

ENEMY INFILTRATES INTO WARDIN, 1230

WARDIN

ENEMY ENTERS WARDIN, 1230

PATROL RETURNS, 1230

SOI-X repulsed, 1400

OUTPOST

1200

1200

1200

TM O'HARA

SOI-X, 1230

SOI-I, 1230

TO BASTOGNE

R. J. KOKE

Map 6

destroyed. The other tanks cleared away from the hill as rapidly as they could. Direct-fire artillery began to hit the force's main position from north across the valley. On the road ahead, the team had hastily set up a minefield. At 1300 a few Germans jumped from a Volkswagen and tried to remove the mines. From only 200 yards away to the west, five of the infantry half-tracks and five medium tanks opened fire on the German party. But they were able to jump in their car and make a clean getaway. Shortly after, an outpost at the south of the position saw another enemy group moving through woods northeast toward Wardin. One of the medium tanks moved up and put them under fire.

These were the things that had happened before the time when Team O'Hara saw men coming toward them from the woods at their rear. These men were in patrol formation and wore an unfamiliar green uniform, which looked tight around the legs. The tankers were just about to fire and then someone in the approaching party yelled. The approaching men were the point of Company I, 501st Parachute Infantry. Their green jump suits had almost been their undoing. The main body of the Company was right behind them in the woods and the company was on its way to Wardin - good news to the tankers. The first infantry support had arrived and they could now withdraw their own patrols which had been reaching out toward the town.

Some fateful minutes passed and nothing was done to unify the action. With the enemy crowding in on them, the forces acted like two ships passing in the night. The paratroopers went on. Two medium tanks were placed so as to cover the exits from Wardin. That was all.

Lieutenant Colonel James O'Hara, commander of the 54th Armored Infantry Battalion, 10th Armored Division, and Team O'Hara of Combat Command B, had thought that the enemy would push west on the Wiltz-Bastogne highway. But he was wrong about it. The Germans bypassed his group - except for a few who squeezed a little too far over to the west and got themselves killed for their pains - and went on to Wardin, moving along a deep gully where O'Hara's tanks couldn't bring their fire to bear. The tankers could see the German infantry infiltrating by twos and threes, moving northwest toward the town, until a hundred or more had passed. They asked that artillery be put on the gully but the Bastogne artillery was occupied with the defense of Noville. Then the enemy began to fret O'Hara's immediate front again: one group came close enough to fire at a tank with a rocket that fell five yards short. Half-tracks sprayed the area with machine-gun fire and the tanks pounded away with their 75mms. Thus preoccupied, Team O'Hara paid no mind to Wardin. They knew there was fighting going on but the situation was "obscure."

At 1415, December 19, Colonel Ewell heard that Company I was being fired on in Wardin. The reports trickling in during the next few minutes indicated that the company was doing pretty well. Armor was now opposing them, but they had already knocked out two tanks and were pushing the enemy infantry from the town. By 1600, Ewell was pretty much content with his general situation. He had three battalions approximately abreast; he was in contact with the enemy all along his front and there was a friendly roadblock - Team O'Hara - on his extreme right flank. But he felt that he had gone as far as he could with his offensive action and that such strength was now being committed against him that he could no longer think about his specific mission (to "seize the road junction at 676614 and hold it.") He therefore ordered his battalions to make plans to break contact at dark and draw back to defend a general line along the high ground to the west of Bizory-Neffe, and in an approximate extension of this line to the southward of the creek. At Division headquarters, General McAulliffe and Colonel Kinnard looked over his plan and approved it.

As he was walking back through Bastogne he met a sergeant from Company I who said to him, "Have you heard about

Company I? We've been wiped out." Ewell got to his radio; he didn't believe the sergeant, but the story was nearer right than he thought. Company I had lost 45 men and 4 officers at Wardin and the survivors had scattered so badly that it was no longer possible to form even a platoon. The news was a shock. When he first heard that Company I was becoming involved in Wardin, Colonel Ewell had ordered it to disengage and withdraw. But before the company could comply, it had come under the full shock of an attack by seven tanks and one infantry battalion from Panzer Lehr. The survivors got out as best they could.

This news simply strengthened Ewell's conviction that he must abandon all further offensive intention and tighten up his position. Colonel O'Hara had reached the same conclusion and for much the same reason. Four of the walking wounded who had gotten out of Wardin had come into his lines and told him the news. He saw his force now in an exposed position with no one on his right, an aggressive enemy on his left and pressure along his whole front, and he asked Combat Command B headquarters for permission to withdraw.

By radio he received his reply, "Contact friends on your left, hold what you have." This told him that headquarters still didn't understand the situation. So he sent his S-3, Captain George A. Renoux, to Bastogne to explain in person what he couldn't with safety discuss over the air, and then went to his rear to reconnoiter a better position. At 1715 he was ordered to withdraw to the high ground north of Marvie - the place he had by then already picked as the best defensive line in the area. The Headquarters Company, Heavy-Weapons Company and engineers were first to start digging into the new slope. When they were in place, the rest of the force came along, except for four medium tanks and one platoon of infantry which covered the withdrawal. Throughout the whole move, the 420th Armored Field Artillery Battalion put a heavy covering fire into, the ground where the enemy had been seen during the day. Not a shot was fired in return.

Because of the loss of Company I and his feeling that the enemy was building up on his right, Colonel Ewell asked Division headquarters to attach one battalion to his regiment for a right flank and reserve. He was given the 1st Battalion of the 327th Glider Infantry under Lieutenant Colonel Hartford F. Salee. They were put in behind Ewell's 3d Battalion which put

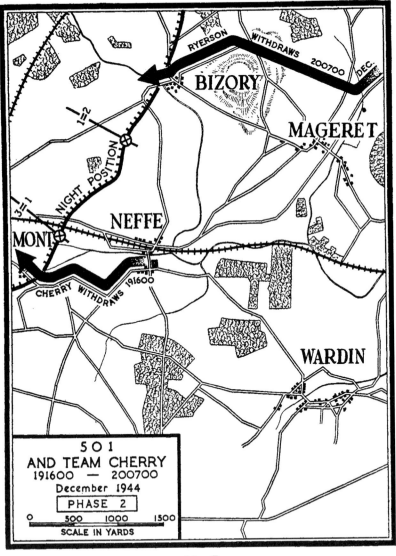

Map 7

them next to Team O'Hara.

Between 1700 and 1800, December 19, the 501st Parachute Infantry fell back to the new defensive line. Estimating his gains and losses, Ewell didn't give his regiment too much credit. He thought that Company I had probably killed some Germans at Wardin, but since the enemy still held the town he couldn't be sure. His impression was that the execution done by his own right and center had not been very great. The honors of the day belonged to the artillery."' Colonel Ewell said, "Any actual killing of the enemy that day was due to the artillery."

Captain Ryerson's force (Company C, 20th Armored Infantry Battalion, 10th Armored Division) of Team Cherry , having spent the day hoping that the infantry would get up to them, clung to three houses in the northwest edge of Magéret after dark. The enemy shot up flares and blazed away at Ryerson's vehicles with antitank guns, destroying three of them. Their infantry then came on but was driven back by the fire of the 420th Armored Field Artillery Battalion.

At 0030, December 20, Combat Command B Headquarters sent orders for Ryerson to withdraw before dawn, and to make contact with Colonel Ewell at Bizory. One line in the special instructions said, "The lead vehicle will inform outpost line of number of vehicles in his column to insure that no Germans follow column into our lines."

Captain Ryerson got ready to move his wounded to a point beyond the crest of the first hill - the first step on the way out.

6. HOLDING THE CHATEAU

COLONEL CHERRY HAD been sitting on the hot seat. Having failed to get to his forward elements the night of December 18, he went to his command post, which was set up in the château 300 yards south of Neffe. A signal company from VIII Corps which had hastily pulled out of this building bad scribbled signs on the walls saying, "We'll be back - The Yanks." One of Cherry's men read it and snorted, "We'll be back - Hell! We're here to stay."

At 0600 on December 19 - just as Ewell's men were passing the initial point - Cherry's Reconnaissance Platoon, 3d Tank Battalion, which was outposting the road junction at Neffe, was hit by enemy tanks and infantry from the east. The platoon knocked out one tank with a bazooka but the enemy kept coming, and after taking some losses, the line broke back under a storm of German rifle, machine-gun and direct artillery fire. Most of the outpost fell back along the Bastogne road up which Major Bottomly's men (1st Battalion, 501st Parachute Infantry) were coming. But three of them were able to get through to Cherry in the château and they carried the word that the enemy had come to Neffe with two tanks and two infantry platoons. *[As this is identical with Major Bottomly's estimate to Colonel Ewell it seems probable that men coming through gave Bottomly his information.]*

At 1000, while Colonel Ewell was committing his 2d Battalion of the 501st, Colonel Cherry saw four more German tanks (one was a Tiger Royal), an armored car and 97 more infantrymen enter Neffe from the direction of Magéret. Right after that they hit his force, and they spent the rest of that day trying to crush him with their left while poking at Ewell's troops with their right. The château was stoutly built and this somewhat compensated for Team Cherry's depleted numbers. Cherry bad to see it through with his headquarters personnel who moved from one side of the building to another as the attack shifted. The automatic weapons had been taken from the vehicles and placed in the windows and at other points where they could cover the château yard and walls. From three sides, the enemy infantry pressed in against the building; the west side of the château was raked with 20mm. and machine-gun fire. *[Since the chateau was west of the German roadblock and the west wall faced toward Major Bottomly, this may have been American fire.]*

But though some died within five yards of the walls, not one German got into the château.

There was only one somber note in the defense. A depleted platoon of engineers, which had arrived from the direction of Mont early in the morning, was ordered to the south of the château at the height of the action. The enemy was moving through woods toward the high ground in that direction. The engineers started on their mission but kept on over the hill and Team Cherry never saw them again. *[There were supposed to be two Engineer roadblocks in the vicinity, one between Bastogne and Neffe and the other at Mont. Colonel Ewell says that he found no engineer group on the Longvilly road. The Mont block was intact when Griswold got there. The group that came to the chateau may have been driven off the Longvilly road by the German fire and after going to the chateau decided to rejoin the other group. The Historian was not able to establish the fact.]*

Some time around mid-afternoon on the 19th a platoon from Ewell's 3d Battalion of the 501st in Mont worked its way carefully forward, taking advantage of the cover afforded by the forest patches and the rise and fall of the ground, and entered the château. *[The work of this party was not known to Colonel Ewell and does not appear in the battalion journal. It appears in the Combat Command B Journal and the Team Cherry interview, and is confirmed in the interview with Colonel Kinnard.]*

It had turned out this way, that whereas the fire of the German tanks had kept Colonel Griswold's 3d Battalion from closing on Neffe, his infantry fire had compelled the Germans to release their tight hold on the château. Too, the enemy must have felt mounting concern for what was occurring on their right. The platoon had come as reinforcements-to help Cherry hold the fort. But by that time the roof was blazing over his head and his men were being smoked out by another fire lighted by German HE shells. *[Such is the confusion of battle that 101st Division command post had the impression that Team Cherry had burned the chateau before withdrawing in order to keep it from falling into enemy hands.]*

He waited until the approach of darkness and then led all hands out of Neffe and back to the infantry lines at Mont.

Before leaving, Colonel Cherry sent Combat Command B this message, "We're not driven out . . . we were burned out. We're not withdrawing . . we are moving."

7. TEAM DESOBRY AT NOVILLE

THE CONTEMPORARY ACCOUNTS which attempted to apportion the credit for the saving of Bastogne had much to say about the 101st Airborne Division and relatively little about any other units. There was irony in the fact that a paratroop outfit which had already done equally brilliant work in Normandy and Holland won world recognition for the first time, and in so doing eclipsed the splendid help given by the other victors, at Bastogne. It was the belief of the commanders at Bastogne that the 28th Infantry Division had absorbed much of the shock of the attack before the enemy reached their front on that first day, and that the harassing of the German flank and rear by the armored forces that had gone out the Longvilly road further lightened the burden upon their own men of the 101st Airborne Division. *[Colonel Roberts also expressed this view on the 28th Division to Westover, but it was not placed in the interview.]*

In those critical hours the armor out along the roads leading north and east was to the infantry in Bastogne like a football end throwing himself in the path of interference so that the secondary defense can have a clean chance to get at the man with the ball.

One of the most desperately placed of these small armored forces was Team Desobry which assembled in the Noville area at 2300 on December 18. The town of Noville is on relatively high ground. Yet it is commanded by two ridges from about 800 yards, one in the southeast and the other running from north to northwest. Because the team arrived in the darkness, full advantage of the natural defenses of the area could not be taken immediately. Major William R. Desobry (Commanding Officer of the 20th Armored Infantry Battalion, 10th Armored Division) set up a perimeter defense of the town under Captain Gordon Geiger of Battalion Headquarters Company. He sent forward three outposts, each consisting of a depleted platoon of infantry and a section of medium tanks. One went east on the Bourcy road, one went northeast on the Houffalize road and the third set up its roadblock at some crosstrails on the road to Vaux. This outpost line was about 800 yards from the main body. The engineers were instructed to install minefields in support of the roadblocks but found it impossible to comply with the order because of the flow of American stragglers back over these same roads. They came on all through the night-men from scattered engineer units, from Combat Command Reserve of the 9th Armored Division and from the 28th Infantry Division. Colonel Roberts had told Major Desobry to draft into his organization any men he could use.

Every vehicle that came down the road was searched for infantry soldiers. Desobry had already decided that he would

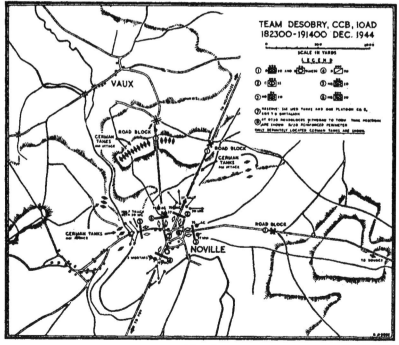

Map 8

incorporate any infantrymen or engineers into the local defense; he needed engineers to set up obstacles. But be ordered his men to let any armored vehicles pass through the lines and continue on to Bastogne. He figured that additional vehicles would merely clog the streets of Noville and increase his vulnerability to enemy artillery fire. The infantry strays came into the line usually in groups of three or four. Many of them had discarded all fighting equipment; few were able to say where they had been; none had maps and none was able to pinpoint the area where he had last seen the Germans. It became the experience of Team Desobry that these stragglers who came to Noville singly or in small groups were of almost no value to the defense; when the action started, they took to the cellars.

This was not true of a platoon of armored infantry from CCR which fell back into Noville near midnight. Their lieutenant had held them together during a running 36-hour fight with enemy armored forces. He gave Major Desobry a vivid picture of his experience and of the action of the enemy forces moving toward Noville from the east. He volunteered to move his platoon into position at Noville and throughout the defense there, it fought courageously.

On the strength of what the lieutenant had told him about the enemy armor, Desobry decided that his own vehicles were overcrowding the village. He ordered the main streets to be cleared and the vehicles to be parked along the side roads. Detailing one officer to stand watch, he then suggested that the rest of the force within the village try to snatch some sleep.

At 0430 on December 19 the flow of stragglers abruptly ceased and Desobry's men grew tense as they waited for an enemy attack. At 0530 a group of half-tracks could be heard and dimly seen approaching the block on the Bourcy road. In the darkness the outpost could not tell whether they were friend or enemy. The sentry to the front yelled "Halt!" four times. The first vehicle pulled to a grinding halt within a few yards of him.

Someone in the half-track yelled something in German. From a bank on the right of the road, Desobry's men showered the half-track with hand grenades. Several exploded as they landed in the vehicle. There was loud screaming as some of the Germans jumped or fell from the half-track and lay in the road. The rest of the enemy column quickly unloaded and deployed in the ditches along the road. There ensued a 20-minute close-up fight with grenades and automatic weapons and although the roadblock crew was greatly outnumbered, the bullet fire did them no hurt because of the protection of the embankment. Staff Sergeant Leon D. Gantt finally decided that too many German potato-mashers were coming into the position and ordered his men to withdraw about 100 yards. At this the Germans turned their half-track around and ran for safety; they were apparently a reconnaissance element and had completed their mission by finding the American outpost. During the action the two tanks had done nothing although they were within 100 yards of the German column. Sergeant Gantt went to Second Lieutenant Allen L. Johnson and asked him why. Johnson replied that he hadn't been sure what to do. He then fired a couple of Parthian shots down the road but the enemy had already disappeared into the fog and darkness. At dawn the outpost fell back on Noville according to instructions.

Twenty minutes after the fighting had died on the Bourcy road three tanks approached the outpost on the Houffalize road. The sound of their motors seemed familiar to Staff Sergeant Major I. Jones who was out by himself some 75 yards in front of the roadblock. He thought they were American. When the tanks were 75 yards away Jones yelled, "Halt!" and fired a quick burst with his BAR over the turret of the lead tank. It stopped 50 yards from him. He heard the occupants conversing in English. Then fire from the tank's caliber .50 broke around Jones' foxhole in the sloping bank on the side of the road. He flattened quickly and the fire missed his back by inches. The men at the roadblock fired on the tanks. Suddenly a cry of "Cease fire, they're friendly troops!" was heard. Jones was not certain whether the cry came from the force in front of him or behind him. The small-arms fire ceased. But the two medium tanks which were supporting the roadblock and were standing about 100 yards from this new armor were less sanguine. The tank on the right side of the road fired its 75mm. The first round hit the bank 15 yards from Jones and almost blew him out of the hole. The foremost tank confronting Jones fired six quick rounds in reply. The first round knocked out the American tank on the right. The second round knocked out the other one. The succeeding rounds also scored direct hits. Yet none of the tankers was killed though several were hard hit. One man had his right leg blown off and his left badly mangled. Private John J. Garry, an infantryman, moved over to the ditch to help the wounded tankers and was hit in the shoulder by a shell fragment.

Jones and the other men in the advanced positions were pinned to their foxholes by the grazing fire from the enemy guns. The American half-tracks were in line behind the Shermans. The position of the ruined armor not only blocked the enemy from coming down the road but gave the half-tracks partial cover so that they could turn their machine guns against the enemy column. A bazooka team tried to get forward but couldn't find a route by which they could bring their rockets to bear. Under these conditions of deadlock the two forces continued to slug it out toe-to-toe while the fog swirled around them and at last closed in so thick that they could scarcely see the muzzle Hashes of the guns. At 0730 the platoon disengaged and withdrew to Noville, acting on the orders given by Major Desobry the night before. They had held to the last minute and so complied with the order, but they were about through in any case, as enemy infantry was now coming up around the flank. The roadblock on the Vaux road was not attacked. But while that party likewise was withdrawing at 0730 they heard die enemy coming down from the north.

During the night of December 18-19 Captain Geiger had set up roadblocks on all roads entering Noville and had placed a thin screen of infantry in a circle just beyond the buildings. The position was particularly weak on the south and west-the sides which the enemy seemed least likely to approach. One tank was posted on the road leading to Bastogne and two were put on the other main exits from the town. In addition, one 57mm. gun and a 75mm. assault gun were placed to cover each of the roads which had been outposted during the night. The survivors of the two opening skirmishes had just drawn back within this defensive circle when 88mm. fire from the northward ripped out of the fog which by this time completely enveloped the village.

From Noville's main street the north-running road is straight for miles. The defenders figured that German tanks were sitting out there on the road somewhere and firing right down the slot. The fire was very heavy for half an hour. It destroyed three half-tracks and a jeep and blew the machine gun from an M8 car. But miraculously, no one was hurt.

At 0830 on the 19th two Tiger tanks nosed out of the fog and stopped within 20 yards of the machine-gun positions covering the northern sector. The 57mm. gun to the right of the road was within 30 yards of the tanks. A medium tank with a 75mm. gun was looking straight at them. The machine gunners alongside the road picked up their bazookas. All fired at the same time and in a second the two Tiger tanks had become just so much wrecked metal. Later, all hands claimed credit for the kill.

A few Germans jumped out of the tanks and started to flee. Machine gunners and riflemen in the outposts cut loose on them. But they could not be sure whether their fire found the targets because the fog swallowed the running men within 30 or 40 yards. Some German infantry had come along behind the tanks and Desobry's men had caught only a glimpse of their figures. But they turned back the moment the skirmish opened.

About 0930 the enemy began to press against the west sector with a series of small probing actions which lasted until 1030. The officer in charge of this ground, Second Lieutenant Eugene E. Todd, was new to action and began to feel that he was sustaining the weight of a major attack by the whole German Army. When he asked Captain Geiger for permission to withdraw, Geiger replied, "Hell, hold your ground and fight." He did.

The real thing started at 1030. The defenders had heard the rumblings of tanks and the puttering of smaller vehicles out in the fog as if a tremendous build-up were going on. Quite suddenly the fog lifted like a curtain going up and revealing the stage. The countryside was filled with tanks. From the second story of his command post in the Noville schoolhouse, Captain Omar R. Billett (Commanding Officer, Company B, 20th Armored Infantry Battalion, 10th Armored Division), saw at a glance more than 30 tanks. Others saw as many more from different points of vantage. In an extended skirmish line along the ridge short of Vaux were 14 tanks. Desobry's men looked at this scene and knew that they were standing square in the road of an entire panzer division. At that moment they might well have uttered the words of Oliver, "Great are the hosts of these strange people, and we have here a very little company," but instead they picked up their arms. The leading enemy formations were 1,000 yards away. The distance made no difference even to the men working with caliber .50 machine guns; they fired with what they bad. When they bad closed to 800 yards out, the 14 tanks on the ridge halted and shelled the town. Other tanks were swinging around the right flank but on the left the enemy armor was already within 200 yards of the American position when the curtain went up.

The events of the next hour were shaped by the flashes of the heavy guns and the vagaries of the ever-shifting fog. The guns rolled in measure according to a visibility that came and went in the passage of only a few seconds. But it never became an infantryman's battle. Little knots of men on foot were coming up behind the German tanks and the batteries of the 420th Armored Field Artillery Battalion hammered at those afoot. It is doubtful if the American artillery stopped a single tank. About the time that the enemy army became fully revealed, a platoon from the 609th Tank Destroyer Battalion rolled into Noville, and added the gunpower of its four tank destroyers to the guns already shooting. The sudden, sharp focus given to the line of Mark IVs and Mark Vs as the fog cleared along the ridge line made them stand out like ducks in a shooting gallery. Nine were hit straightaway, three exploding in flames. One came charging down the highway and was turned into a flaming wreck 500 yards out. At a range of 600 yards an American cavalryman engaged a Panther tank with his armored car and knocked it out with one shot from his 37mm. gun-the most miraculous hit of the morning.

Two tanks that had been close in the foreground, ahead of the ridge, also charged the town at a speed that brought momentary confusion to Desobry's command post. But at 30 yards' range, a 105mm. assault gun fired its first round, stopping one tank, but not disabling its gun. The German fired but missed, then tried to withdraw, but with a quick round the assault gun finished him off. The other German tank had been stopped by one of Desobry's mediums at a range of 75 yards. Looking in the direction from which they had come, observers in the taller buildings of Noville could see four more tanks lying in a draw-almost concealed. The ground cover was good enough so the Noville guns. couldn't get at them-until one of these tanks made the mistake of pulling out onto the road. It was a shining mark, 300 yards away. A tank destroyer fired and the tank exploded in a blaze. The fog swirled back, screening the draw, and the other three tanks ran off into it.

To the east of town, the run down the flank by the enemy

armor ended with the destruction of three of the tanks. German infantry had appeared on that side in fairly large numbers, but when the lifting of the fog exposed them, they turned and ran, and bullet fire from Noville thinned their ranks while they were running. In Noville, the defending infantry company had lost 13 wounded; four of our vehicles had been wrecked and one tank destroyer smashed-mainly from indirect artillery fire with which the Germans had harassed the town as their tanks came on.

By 1130 the fight had died, though intermittent shelling continued to worry the garrison.3A Its effect on Desobry had been as Colonel Roberts had predicted on the night before. The sudden lifting of the fog and revelation of the enemy position had made him acutely conscious that the conditions of ground imposed an inordinate handicap on his own force. From their positions along the ridges on three sides of Noville, the Germans could put their tanks in hull defilade and keep the village under a close artillery fire until all the walls were leveled. Desobry could see nothing but disaster ahead if be tried to hold the present ground. He figured he had better withdraw, but at the same time he remembered the counsel that Colonel Roberts had given him. In mid-morning, at the height of the German attack, he called Roberts and asked for permission to withdraw to the high ground around the village of Foy.

This was an act of near fatal consequences though in the end it saved the situation. What happened was that at Major Desobry's CP no effort was made to keep the message secret from all save its handlers. The operator spoke loudly and all others in the command post heard what he said. The word spread quickly to the troops out on the fighting line. In the course of the action these vague rumors hardened into a positive report that the command had received permission for a withdrawal to Foy. The wish had fathered the thought; the intensifying of the German fire made it very easy to believe. Groups of armored infantrymen - and nearly all of the stragglers who had been plugging gaps in the line - came drifting back into Noville; they had heard the story and had quit their foxholes. It seemed to Desobry that his line was about to disintegrate. He rallied his command post officers and noncoms and they began working frantically with these groups, bullying them, swearing that the rumor was false and turning them back to the action.

Reluctantly the men faced back toward the enemy but others kept on coming. There was no end to the problem. That one lapse in the CP kept the team off balance during the deadliest part of the day. Yet Desobry noted that his subordinates were accepting even these extra odds cheerfully. From the commander on down, not a man had any idea of the over-all importance of the engagement; it was just another local affair and they had scarcely related it even to the defense of Bastogne. What buoyed their spirits was that the Germans were coming in with their chins down; their own armor was remaining open. The difference was telling clearly in the marksmanship of the two sides and in the comparative losses in fighting vehicles. Every fair hit on an enemy tank produced a lift of enthusiasm for the fight partly offsetting the ill effect of the withdrawal rumor. Not all of those who drifted back to the village were bent on withdrawal; some came for just a moment to boast of what they had done to the enemy in their sector and then to return to their work again. Witnessing this strangely disordered contest and catching its wild notes of dismay and triumph, Major Desobry was reminded of a barroom brawl. His concern, however, was not solely due to the power of the German attack. That morning he had sent patrols out to reconnoiter his rear and the patrols had not returned.

Colonel Roberts sparred with the request from Noville. He still possessed authority to sanction the withdrawal of his own elements but he reckoned that the situation required steadfastness for the time being and until the 101st Division was solidly established in Bastogne. So at first he gave no answer.

He left his own CP and started for General McAuliffe's headquarters to see what could be done. Before he had gone halfway he ran into Brigadier General Higgins, assistant division commander of the 101st. Even as he rapidly sketched the situation to Higgins (the time was 1050) the 1st Battalion of 506th Parachute Infantry, under Lieutenant Colonel James L. LaPrade, passed by in the street. At the head of the regimental column, accompanying LaPrade, was the 506th's commander, Colonel Robert F. Sink. Convinced by Roberts' words that the Noville situation was fully desperate, Higgins on the spot ordered Sink to send a battalion to Noville and LaPrade automatically drew the assignment.

[McAuliffe likewise says that LaPrade was sent to Noville because of Desobry's predicament.]

Colonel Sink was further directed that his 2d and 3d Battalions should be put in Division reserve just north of Bastogne on the Noville road. At the same time the 1st Battalion, which had been given the Noville mission, was detached from Regiment and put under Division control. Colonel Roberts returned to his CP and called Major Desobry. "You can use your own judgment about withdrawing," he said, "but I'm sending a battalion of paratroopers to reinforce you."

Desobry replied, "I'll get ready to counterattack as soon as possible."

Colonel LaPrade and his staff got up to Major Desobry at 1130 and told him the battalion was on the way. It was not quite clear to either of the local commanders whether there had been an attachment of one force to the other but they decided that for the time being they would keep it a "mutual affair." Colonel LaPrade and his command had just one 1:100,000 map to serve them for the forthcoming operation.

The commanders agreed that the next order of business was to attack due north and seize the high ground the enemy had tried to use as a springboard during the morning. Infantry and armor would jump off together at 1400. However, Colonel LaPrade's battalion didn't arrive until 1330 and couldn't get ready that soon. So the jumpoff was postponed until 1430, December 19, since meanwhile there was a small matter of supply to be finally adjusted.

The 506th Parachute Infantry had left Mourmelon in such a hurry that many of the men did not have helmets and others were short of weapons and ammunition. Colonel LaPrade told Major Desobry about this embarrassment and the armored force's S-4, Second Lieutenant George C. Rice, was sent packing to Foy to bring up ammunition. On the way he met the upcoming 1st Battalion and asked for their supply officer; but this officer was in Bastogne beating the woods for weapons and ammunition. So Lieutenant Rice asked the company officers what they needed most, and found that rocket launchers, mortars and all types of ammunition were the critical shortages. He then dashed on to Foy and loaded the jeep with cases of hand grenades and M1 ammunition. The jeep was turned around and the stuff was passed out to the paratroopers as they marched. On his next shuttle, Rice got back to the moving, battalion with a jeep and a truck overloaded with weapons and ammunition. The materiel was put alongside the road in five separate piles so that the men could pick up the things they needed as they went by. He made one more trip and caught the head of the column just before it reached the limits of Noville. A load of 81 mm. mortar ammunition came into town after the battalion got there.

These details caused a slight delay in getting the battle under way again.

8. ATTACK AND WITHDRAWAL

COLONEL LAPRADE and Major Desobry wanted the high ground and this was their plan-that three tanks would strike northward along the Houffalize road and four tanks would hit east toward the high ground west of Bourcy. With this group of tanks would go one and one-half platoons of infantry for their close-in support. In between these two armored groups moving along the road, LaPrade's paratroopers would spread themselves over the middle ground. One company would advance south over the Bourcy road, another off to the left of it would extend to the Houffalize road and the third company would go toward the high ground at Vaux. In this way, armor and infantry would spread out fanwise as they left Noville and started for the commanding ridges.

However, the preliminaries were not propitious. Noville was already taking a pounding from the enemy artillery. The Germans were firing by the clock and dropping twenty to thirty shells into the defensive position every ten minutes. The houses and several of the vehicles were afire. A proper reconnaissance became impossible; the assembly went off badly. Still, the attack got away at 1430, December 19, though somewhat unsteadily.

The line had scarcely moved out from the houses when an artillery concentration landed in the middle of Company C of the 506th Parachute Infantry, which was on the right flank.3 A number of men were hit but the company kept moving. Bullet fire from enemy positions on the high ground bit into the infantry ranks and slowed their advance. The little groups worked their way along, dashing on to favorable ground, stopping there to fire, then making a rush on to the next point of cover.

But elsewhere along the line, except on the far left where

Company B kept moving, the attack was already flagging. The tanks and armored infantry decided the attack was impossible so moved back to their holes, not even realizing that the paratroopers were continuing to attack in any strength. Company A was blocked by heavy tank fire immediately and after a small advance was forced to return to the village. But on the flanks, B and C went on until they reached the lower slopes of the objective ridges and started to climb. At that moment the enemy tanks came against them, supported by some infantry. A few of the paratroopers kept going; their snow-covered bodies were found on the ridges weeks later. *[Backed by statements made to Westover in an interview with battalion officers on March 13, 1945.]*

But the greater part of the two companies went to earth and sought whatever cover was at hand. Then they continued to slug it out with their small arms as best they could. They could hardly see the enemy at any time. The fog was closing down again and

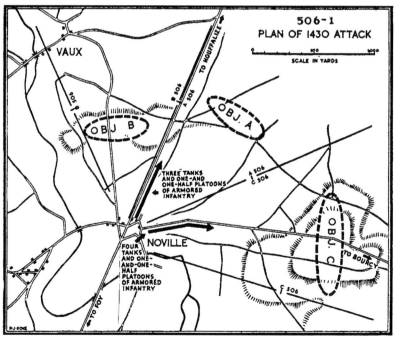

Map 9

it was mixed with the smoke drifting over from the fires of Noville.

They held the ground until dark. Then Colonel LaPrade's men fell back on Noville. The fighting on the slopes had cost the battalion heavily but the men thought they had caused equal losses to the enemy. From the town itself three tank destroyers had exchanged fire at about 1500 yards with the enemy tanks and had kept them from coming on. But whether they had done any real hurt to them could not be seen.

[506th Parachute Infantry claims that five of these tanks were destroyed but the statement is considered insufficient because proofs were lacking and in view of the conditions already described.]

For about an hour after the return to Noville the front was deathly quiet. LaPrade's men-had had no chance to dig in prior to the attack so they sought refuge in the houses. Colonel LaPrade improved his command post by moving a heavy clothes closet in front of the window. *[From statement by Harwick to Marshall. This statement was never committed to writing because it was made in answer to a question prior to an interview which was to be held at a later hour. Before the interview could be held Harwick was hit.]*

The Germans resumed their bombardment of the town and in the middle of the shelling a platoon of tank destroyers from the 706th Tank Destroyer Battalion reported for duty. Further tightening the defense, General Higgins, having arrived at Noville just as the American counterattack was fading, took the essential steps toward unifying the local command. Major Desobry and Colonel LaPrade were in agreement that one man should be in control, and LaPrade, being the senior, drew the assignment. LaPrade told General Higgins that he thought he could hold on until dark but that he was convinced that the enemy would attack in strength shortly thereafter. Soon after that, Colonel Sink got up to Noville for a personal reconnaissance. He talked to LaPrade and the latter shortly issued his orders for the combined defense. The plan was for Company B to defend to the northwest and Company A to the northeast and Company C was to cover the southern half of the perimeter while the armored group was held in the center of the town ready to strike out in any direction.14 A few minutes after LaPrade was placed in command, an 88 shell landed in the street outside the command post. The explosion shattered the clothes closet and both commanders were struck down by fragments. Colonel LaPrade was killed and Major Desobry wounded. Major Robert F. Harwick, LaPrade's executive, who had rushed back from a leave in Paris to join his battalion and had arrived in Noville just at the close of the afternoon fighting, took command of the combined force. The armor passed into the hands of Major Charles L. Hustead.

For the men of Combat Command B who were within the town the rest of the night (December 19-20) was comparatively quiet. Their peace was punctured at times by the dropping of a few artillery shells and out beyond the wall of fog they could hear the noise of an enemy build-up. There was little quiet, however, along the infantry perimeter. Enemy tanks in twos and threes, supported by infantry, probed toward them. When warned by small-arms or bazooka fire, they checked and blazed away at the positions from which they had seen the flashes. The accompanying Germany infantry tried to infiltrate through the lines. These small penetrations and the resulting fire were such that it was almost impossible to maintain wire communication with the outposts. For the paratroopers those hours were a nightmare of surprise fire, ominous noise and confusion. But when morning came the light revealed that two of the enemy tanks had been knocked out by bazooka fire.

These opening blows in the first round at Noville had been enough to convince General McAuliffe that the enemy was full of fight. After that first day they would never seem as strong to him again and the impression would deepen that their attacks were coming on in diminishing volume. But on the first day he looked toward his northern sector with increasing concern. In the afternoon of December 19, the 3d Battalion of 506th had been ordered to move up to Foy between Bastogne and Noville and establish a line there, with the 2d Battalion moving to Luzery as a regimental reserve. When this move was made, Company H on the right made contact with the 501st Parachute Infantry by patrol and Company G on the left joined with the 502d Parachute Infantry, maintaining a strong point in Recogne. That night all platoons of Company C of the 705th Tank Destroyer Battalion were attached to the 506th Parachute Infantry and General McAuliffe got ready to employ as much of the strength of 502d along his northern flank as the morrow would prove necessary.

This small, confused action had reverberated all the way back to Corps. On returning to Bastogne, Higgins had reported to McAuliffe as follows: "I think we're way out on a limb. There is too much distance between LaPrade in Noville and Strayer in Foy. It is my judgment that the Noville force had better get out."

Colonel Sink, having carried out his independent reconnaissance, had reached exactly the same conclusion. At around 1820 he called Division and said that it was getting very hot at Noville; he urged that his forward battalion be withdrawn to a point north of Foy. But in view of the fact that General Middleton had ordered that Noville be defended and that the armor which had gone forward in response to that direction was still acting under Roberts's orders, it looked like a matter for decision by the higher headquarters. General McAuliffe called General Middleton and relayed Higgins's and Sink's reports of the situation, adding his personal recommendation that the force be withdrawn. Middleton said, "No; if we are to hold on to Bastogne, you cannot keep falling back." Sink was called and told that the Noville force would have to stick. By then, Major

Desobry had ceased to worry about the local problem. He was unconscious when they removed him from the CP to the nearest field hospital. He was still out, when, a few hours later, the Germans overran the hospital and took him prisoner.

9. DOUBTS AND DECISIONS

YET ON THE WHOLE, that first night in Bastogne, the situation was good, and it was largely the intuition and hunch and driving energy of the leaders that had made it so. The day of the 19th had proved that in the few minutes allowed him the night before, General McAuliffe had sized up the position properly.

[Examination of the assembly area overlay alongside of how the battle developed makes this fact self-evident. However there was considerable discussion between General McAuliffe and the Historian which is not included in the notes. General McAuliffe said that when the siege was over he felt that his choice of the assembly area was one of his most fortunate decisions and that he would not have altered it in any way looking at battle retrospectively. He said that he had not given a great deal of thought to the situation before making his decision but that he "felt" that the area selected was the right place.]

He had been tossed into a battle in which nearly all the major facts about the movement of forces were either unknown or obscure. He had rejected Corps' idea that the 101st Airborne Division be assembled to the southwest of Bastogne. It was a point that didn't give particular concern to General Middleton so long as General McAuliffe got his troops in where they were best placed to defend the town. However, VIII Corps Headquarters' reasoning was based on the long-range thought that after the enemy found he could not get through Bastogne, his next important move would be to the southwest. In his hasty reconnaissance out to the westward with Colonel Kinnard, his G-3, late in the day on the 18th, General McAuliffe had selected the ground for his camp from the short-range point of view. He wanted an assembly area which would place him at maximum advantage with respect to his own immediate deployments and the movements of the enemy in the immediate future. Though he had no way of knowing it at the time, his center of equilibrium was on the ground farthest removed from the early dangers of the encirclement although his two eastward-facing regiments were pointed directly toward the avenues along which the Germans would make their first approaches. The first day's results proved that the angels had been with him as he made his first decisions.

In the opening arrangements one decision was taken which worked out adversely. Lieutenant Colonel David Gold, the surgeon of the 101st Division, and Lieutenant Colonel Carl W. Kohls, the Division supply officer, had picked out a conveniently located crossroads to the westward of the Division assembly area and decided that this must be the rear, if there were such a thing. The Division hospital was set up on the crossroads. Near

Wounded in the hospitals of Bastogne had to lie on the floors because of a lack of equipment.

A trailer is loaded with parachutes for use in the improvised hospitals in Bastogne.

midnight of December 19 the 327th Glider Infantry was told to send a motorized patrol to crossroads X - the site of this evacuation center. The patrol was to investigate and clear up reports of machine-gun fire in that vicinity. They encountered no fire but the hospital was gone - Colonel Gold and all his officers and the men of the clearing company had been captured by the enemy. The 327th patrol decided that there must have been a fight, for dead Germans dressed in civilian clothes were found strewn over the ground, though there were no bodies of American soldiers. The bulk of the Division medical supplies had been captured or destroyed.

Division then called on VIII Corps for medical help, and all 101st Division units were notified that casualties would be evacuated to the aid station of the 501st Parachute Infantry in Bastogne itself. One platoon of the 429th Medical Collecting Company, then located at Jodenville (about one mile west of Sibret), was made available to the 101st. Until the night of

December 21 the platoon used its five ambulances and two weapons carriers to carry some of the wounded back to the 635th Medical Clearing Company. Then the Germans cut across the road and contact was lost with the clearing unit. An abandoned medical supply dump and the chance discovery of another depot in Bastogne containing blankets, litters, splint baskets and other hospital items helped the situation. Yet there continued to be a critical shortage of bed clothing, litters, penicillin, surgical instruments and surgeons.

The losses of the first day of battle had not, however, put any unusual stress on the medical facilities. But later in the fight when Bastogne became encircled, many of the wounded would have to lie on concrete floors with little or no cover. The blankets of the dead were collected so that there would be a chance for the living, and the shattered homes of Bastogne were searched for any kind of quilting.

Colonel W. L. Roberts, commanding Combat Command B, 10th Armored Division, had been at Château-Thierry in 1918 and he well remembered the things that happen during the rout of an army. In his first conversation with General Middleton in which the VIII Corps commander had outlined the missions that sent the three combat teams of Combat Command B to Wardin, Longvilly and Noville on the night of December 18, Colonel Roberts had foreseen one of the main problems.

General Middleton said to him, "The 28th Infantry Division and the 9th Armored are ahead of us. They are badly cut up. The situation is fluid."

Colonel Roberts replied, "Sir, there will be stragglers. I want authority to use these men."

Middleton agreed orally and later confirmed it with a written message: "Major General Middleton directs that you have authority to take over all or any part of Reserve Command, 9th Armored Division, in case they show the slightest inclination to retire. Anything you do to prevent falling back in that area will be given fullest backing."

Colonel Roberts set his net to catch those drifting back. His Headquarters Company was instructed to keep hot food ready all day at a central point in Bastogne. A detail stood by to get these men from other units into billets around the town square. MPs were stationed at the road crossings in the south of Bastogne with instructions to stop every soldier who was trying to get away from the battle and turn him back to the Combat Command B area. About 250 stragglers were thus reorganized in Bastogne on December 19. Some were men from the 9th Armored; most were from the 28th Division. In this way Team Snafu was born, and within the next week it came to include 600 men, led by casual officers; but this outfit was severely handicapped by the fact that they were short of equipment and transportation as long as the siege lasted. Team Snafu was mainly a reservoir for the defending force. The stragglers went into it, the regular units drew from it as they had need.

Any organized units heading south were also commandeered. At 1400 on December 19 the 73d Armored Field Artillery Battalion of Combat Command Reserve, 9th Armored, moved through Bastogne. Colonel Roberts watched it go by before suddenly realizing that it was his for the taking. He sent a staff officer to bring the battalion back and within a few minutes the battalion commander reported at his command post. Roberts told him to put the battalion in position with the 420th Armored Field Artillery Battalion. The commander returned to his battalion but found that there was insufficient fuel for his vehicles and could not make the return trip. The 58th Armored Field Artillery Battalion was stopped and put into position with the 420th, where its twelve guns fired during the next day. Just before the Germans closed the roads to the southward, this unit heard that it had been cut off from Bastogne so it moved to the west. The 771st Field Artillery Battalion - a Negro unit - was commandeered on December 21 and their 155mm. howitzers gave body to the artillery throughout the siege. Colonel Roberts also found in Bastogne eight new undelivered tanks, complete with their Ordnance crews, and he inducted them forthwith into his organization.

Colonel Roberts had worried a lot about the security of the town itself for he had only part of his Engineer battalion and the Antiaircraft Artillery battalion as reserve. General McAuliffe wanted to keep his own reserve as mobile as possible and couldn't see assigning one of his battalions to garrison the town. A task force from Combat Command B, 9th Armored Division, entered Bastogne to learn the situation but was ordered by higher authority to withdraw to Leglise, six miles southeast of Neufchâteau. A request to 10th Armored for the use of the Reserve Command was turned down. So finally Colonel Roberts committed Team Snafu, under command of Captain Charles Brown of 110th Infantry, to the close-in defense of Bastogne. Team Snafu's complexion was somewhat changed on e following morning, December 20, when Brigadier General George A. Davis of the 28th Division arrived in Bastogne with a request that Combat Command B attack toward Wiltz. It couldn't be done, for by that hour all of Colonel Roberts' forces were fully committed. Not long after General Davis departed, Combat Command B was ordered by Corps to release all 28th Division stragglers to their own command. *[Colonel Roberts said he was very sorry to see these men go.]*

Throughout the first day of battle there had been losses and a few minor gains in the 101st Division's already strained supply situation. In the 907th Glider Field Artillery Battalion, Lieutenant Colonel Nelson, worried because his ammunition supply was rapidly reaching the vanishing point, dispatched searching convoys toward what he thought was the Division rear. They moved westward and had been gone about six hours before Colonel Nelson grew aware that he had actually sent his trucks into enemy ground and that they were cut off. A second convoy of five trucks and trailers was sent toward Neufchâteau under Staff Sergeant Vincent Morgan, a supply sergeant. Sergeant Morgan was told that if he could not get M3 ammunition (standard for the 105mm. M3, a gun especially adapted for glider use) he was to bring back some M2 ammunition which the manual said could be used in an emergency.

[The substitute ammunition proved quite satisfactory. According to Nelson its close-up position enabled Baker Battery to make more effective use of the M2 ammunition. The observers had remained with the forward platoons and this was true of most of the Bastogne operation with the result that casualties among forward observers ran very high. Nelson lost four observers killed. Many of the missions therefore had to be adjusted by infantry observers and Nelson said that the results were generally excellent. Due to atmospheric conditions the greater part of the adjustments had to be made by sound. When observation permitted time fire was used with good results.]

The fortitude with which this young noncom carried out his assignment was one of the finest things of the siege. He returned late that night through heavy shelling and small-arms fire about one hour before the Germans cut the road of his inbound journey. He bad first gone to Neufchâteau and on being disappointed there he had driven far to the northwestward, covering in all about 75 miles. On his trucks were 1,500 rounds of M2. It was the only resupply of ammunition received by the 101st Airborne Division before the air resupply came in.

[Most of the supply points listed in VIII Corps' Administrative Orders Nos. 39 and 40 of December 18 and December 19 were either in enemy hands or had been moved to the rear by the hour the orders were received. VIII Corps radioed G-4 one time that there were 7,000 or more rounds of 75mm. howitzer ammunition in the abandoned ammunition supply point No. 128. G-4 asked where that depot was located but never received a reply. On December 20, Captain Salve H. Matheson, S-4 of the 506th

Parachute Infantry, drove to St. Hubert and to Bellauz in a fruitless search for small-arms ammunition. Major William C. Young, 101st Division Artillery S-4, reported that both the ammunition officer and the artillery officer of Corps said that the nearest ammunition supply point which had 105mm. M3 ammunition was Audun le Roman, which is in the south of Luxembourg. The 101st Division also received the slightly ironic information that a train loaded with ammunition of all the types desired by the 101st was being unloaded at Bertrix.]

That partly compensated for a stroke of bad luck. The two convoys of the Division Quartermaster and Ordnance companies reached the Division rear area late at night and were told to remain at a crossroads in the woods (P448630). Lacking time in which to reconnoiter the area, the two companies left all trucks parked on highway N4 facing west. Shortly after midnight on December 20, Division headquarters was notified that the service area was receiving machine-gun fire, and a few minutes later came the message "Evidence indicates service troops have disappeared."

That alarm was enough; within five minutes a message was on its way to Corps headquarters asking for Quartermaster and Ordnance help.

After being flushed by the fire the two companies had headed west and then south. Most of the trucks got through to the Corps rear and on the next day Captain John L. Patterson of one of the units, the 801st Ordnance Maintenance Company, taking a different route, got into Bastogne with two trucks bringing 500 gallons of gasoline. He then turned south again to bring the rest of the convoy forward. But by that time the Germans had already closed the road.

Such was the shortage of gasoline in Bastogne through most of the siege that vehicles were fueled only just before they went out on a run so that there would be no loss of gasoline if any standing vehicle was hit.

10. THE REPULSE

IT WAS A NIGHT FOR DRIFTERS, the night of December 19-20. As the darkness grew, more men from the elements which had been shattered to the east of Bastogne came moving back through the regimental lines of the 101st. Few of them stayed. Colonel Ewell and his officers talked to these men. They could tell very little of what had happened to them. Many of them were inarticulate. Infantrymen from units of the 28th Division still trickled into the area in groups of three or four. They made no attempt to organize themselves and they did not for the most part wish to be organized by anyone else. Some of these straggling infantrymen would ask Ewell's men, "What are you doing?" Upon being told, "We are fighting Germans," they would look at the paratroopers as if they were stark mad.

But not all were like that. Some who seemed utterly wretched and spent when they came to within the lines, upon being handed a K ration, would eat it and look around and ask where they could get a rifle. They were ready to fight again. But to others food and companionship made no difference. They had been shocked so badly that they wanted only to keep on drifting. They were allowed to do so. This disorder had no ill effect on the combat force. The demoralization did not seem to bother the nerves of the men who were still fighting and they accepted it as the natural product of battle it often is.

[However, the Historian talked to perhaps a dozen of Colonel Ewell's officers to gather their general impression of how the stragglers acted and how the combat force reacted and all statements were to the same point.]

A battalion of Field Artillery, the 109th of the 28th Division, came through as a unit and attached itself to the 907th Glider

Field Artillery Battalion. Those groups from the 9th Armored Division which had been compelled to withdraw from the advanced ground along the Longvilly road were in good order and high spirits when they reached the lines around Bastogne. One platoon of armored infantry attached itself to Major Homan's battalion (2d Battalion, 501st Parachute Infantry) and helped them carry the fight during the next several days. Seven tanks arrived from the 9th Armored Division and constituted themselves a small task force operating in support of the

A 75mm M1A1 howitzer being fired by paratroop artillery-men during the siege of Bastogne.

battalion. At 0200 the 2d Platoon of Company B, 705th Tank Destroyer Battalion arrived with four tank destroyers and took position on the south edge of Bizory.

These reinforcements got there in the nick of time. At 0530, December 20, while the 501st Parachute Infantry was patrolling toward its front, the 2d Battalion got an attack over the same big hill to the east of Bizory where they bad been stopped by the German reconnaissance force the day before. At a range of 3,000 yards, the tank destroyer men saw six enemy tanks rolling toward them from the southeast. Sergeant Floyd A. Johnson led his section to the bill north of Bizory and put the two tank destroyers on either side of the road. First Lieutenant Frederic Mallon led the second section to the higher ground southeast of town and waited for the German tanks in an open field.

The firing opened at 0730, the tank destroyers withholding their fire from the enemy infantry so as not to compromise an engagement with the enemy armor, which by this time comprised one Mark IV, one Mark V and two 75mm. self-propelled guns. *[This disagrees with Colonel Ewell's statement of force engaged but Ewell said he was uncertain of the facts.]*

These were following the infantry line by 400 yards - it was a full battalion of infantry, the 2d of the 76th Regiment, 26th Volksgrenadier Division . In the first long-range exchange of fire, one tank destroyer was disabled and its loader killed by a direct hit on the turret; it limped away to the rear. The second tank destroyer in this section, after knocking out the Mark IV tanks, pulled back into Bizory where, in taking up another position, it damaged the tube of its gun by running against a building and became incapacitated. The other tank destroyer section opened fire at 600 yards on the Mark IV tank and one self-propelled gun, destroying both.

This was the crux of the engagement: most of the in-fighting of that morning of December 20 was done by the heavy guns. Major Homan's machine guns had opened up on the German

↑ HOUFFALIZE 7½ MI.

Situation 20 Dec 1944

① RYERSON'S FORCE WITHDRAWS FROM MAGERET 0630. 501 HEAVILY ATTACKED DURING DAY & AT 1400.

② TEAM HUSTEAD & 506-1 WITHDRAW FROM NOVILLE. 506 REGT ENGAGED AT FOY.

③ ENEMY ATTACKS MARVIE AT 1123.

④ NEUFCHATEAU ROAD CUT BY ENEMY.

Mabompre

Bertogne

MARCHE 18 MI.

SPRIMONT ½ MI.

ST.HUBERT 10 MI.

Vaux TEAM H

2PGR   2 PZ (-)

502
506

B   10

Noville   Bourcy

Longchamps

Foy

Champs

506

304

ST.VITH 21 MI.

Flamierge

501 TEAM C

28 RCN

Mande St Etienne

101

B   10

Longvilly

BASTOGNE

B   10   Bizory   Mageret

116 PZ

Senonchamps

Mont   TEAM D   Neffe

901 PGR

Chenogne

B   10

Wardin

Marvie

902

Villeroux

Magerotte

Sibret

ST.HUBERT 10 MI

Assenois   Remoifosse

Morhet

9   5

130 PZ LEHR (-)

Clochimont

NEUFCHATEAU 10 MI

ARLON 20 MI

WILTZ 7 MI.

0   1,000

SCALE IN YARDS

Map 10

infantry while the tanks were coming on and by so doing bad kept them at a distance. Within a few minutes of this first body check to the German battalion, all the artillery that General McAuliffe could turn eastward from Bastogne blasted them. Homan's infantry along the ridge was too far distant to do much bullet damage to the advancing German formations but his men had a clear view of the German ranks coming on slowly, of the automatic fire making them hesitate, of the shells falling among them, of the attack gradually spending itself and of the enemy that was left then breaking away to the northward to escape the fire.

Colonel Ewell's own infantry losses were almost nothing, but two tank destroyers were out of action for the time being and the defense had also lost two tanks. So ended the first, though not the most ruinous, of the piecemeal efforts which on this day presaged the failure of the German battle. This particular fighting had lasted about two hours, the artillery barrage perhaps twenty minutes. *[The 501st Parachute Infantry had no record of when action ended.]*

Prisoners-of-war letters captured from the 76th Regiment said that their losses had been terrible.

There followed a day-long wait along Colonel Ewell's 501st Parachute Infantry front. About 1900 the Germans put a heavy shelling from tanks and self-propelling guns on sensitive points over the ground held by the 501st-Bizory, Mont and the road junctions. The bombardment severed all the telephone wires connecting the battalions with the rear.

As the German artillery slacked off, the 1st Battalion of the 501st radioed to Ewell that the enemy was charging straight down the road from Neffe. Major Raymond V. Bottomly's 1st Battalion could hear the tanks coming on but it was so dark that they could tell little else. All the guns from the eleven artillery battalions in Bastogne dropped a dam of fire across the road one or two hundred yards west of Neffe - the heaviest and most effective American defensive fire during the siege. Three German tanks, two of them Panthers and one a Tiger Royal, were hit and destroyed just as they drew past the last houses in the village. Some German infantry, which had moved down the Bastogne road before the barrage dropped, met their fate from machine guns Company B had posted in a house by the side of the road. That company took the shock without having to yield one yard of ground. Their strongpoint controlled the terrain so well that not one German drew near enough to close on the infantry line. They were killed to the last man, and for weeks later, their grotesque forms along the roadside, heaped over by the Ardennes snows, showed where the German death march ended. The most forward of these bodies was 300 yards ahead of the shattered tanks.

The German thrust from Neffe coincided with an assault on

the 3d Battalion's position at Mont, though here the battle took a quite different form because of Major Templeton's tank destroyers. *[Ewell was convinced that the presence of the tank destroyers made this change.]*

The 1st Platoon of Company B, 705th Tank Destroyer Battalion, under command of First Lieutenant Robert Andrews, had arrived to reinforce Colonel Griswold's 3d Battalion position on the evening of December 19. One tank destroyer was posted at the bend in the road. From here it could cover both the dirt road winding across the valley from Neffe and a draw leading off to the southward. A second tank destroyer took position by the last house, which put it somewhat behind, but in line with, the tank destroyer blocking the Neffe road. The other section was placed on the north side of Mont to check any tank advance from directly across the valley. The tank destroyers held these positions until the hour came when they were most needed, on the night of December 20.

Between 1900 and 1930 on that night the enemy struck through the fields lying between Neffe and Mont, advancing against Colonel Griswold's left. But the presence of the tank destroyers had intimidated the German armor. It took refuge in the little wood lying just west of the Neffe château and from the grove it shelled Mont. The German infantry advanced under this fire. Enemy self-propelled guns moved along the railway line from Neffe a short distance (the rails here ran through a cut) and went to work on the same target. These two lines of fire converged on Griswold's positions at almost a right angle; the men in the forward line had to give ground, falling back on the village. The most forward of the tank destroyers, commanded by Sergeant George N. Schmidt, became their rallying point. Schmidt unloaded most of his crew and told them to join the fight with small arms. He then joined the infantry machine gunners who were already searching the down slopes with every automatic gun the Battalion could bring to bear; in the next few

On the night of December 20, the enemy struck at the left flank of the 3d Battalion, 501st Parachute Infantry). This scene from the outskirts of Neffe shows the enemy preparing for the attack. The American position is on the crest of the hill to the left. The little village of Mont is in the center draw, and the barbed-wire fences, so costly to the enemy, are to the right of the pine grove.

minutes be threw 2,000 rounds of caliber .50 at the enemy. Lieutenant Andrews used a radio-equipped jeep as his command post and central control station, and used his security section as ammunition carriers to feed the stuff up to whichever tank destroyer was calling for it most urgently. The other three tank destroyers, under Sergeant Darrell J. Lindley, were shooting at the railway line. They tried at first to spot the self-propelled guns by firing at muzzle blasts; when that failed, they put flares up over the valley.

The fighting died about 2300. By that time, the three self-propelled guns were out, and lines of German dead littered the hillside. Because of the dark the defenders of Mont had no clear idea of why their automatic fire had made such a clean reaping of the German attack or of where the attack had broken. But in the light of the next morning, December 21, they could see what had happened. The hillside between Neffe and Mont is crossed in both directions by barbed-wire fences spaced between thirty and fifty yards apart, with five or six strands in each fence. In ordinary times they were used, apparently, as feeder pens for cattle. With the tank fire behind them the Germans tried to come right through this fenced area without first destroying the fences in any way or equipping infantry to cut them. On coming to the fences they tried to climb through but the spaces were small and their individual equipment was bulky. Griswold's men bad perfectly clear fields of fire and so did the tank destroyer supporting them. The fences were as effective as any entanglement. The evenly spaced lines of dead told the story. They had charged right into a giant mantrap.

Colonel Ewell had the impression that night that the 901st Panzer Regiment had about expended itself and that it could no longer muster enough men to be an effective offensive force. They bad been somewhat roughly handled before they got to Neffe and his own men furthered the good work.

So on December 19 the Germans, having gained contact with

the 501st Parachute Infantry on a wide front, at first drew back to defensive positions. On December 20 the enemy made three attacks and the infantry, armor and tank destroyers in Colonel Ewell's sector beat them all down. One of these fights was tactically less spectacular but strategically more useful than the others.

During the period of the fighting at Noville and Neffe there had been an action between the flanks of the 501st and 506th Parachute Infantry regiments which, although just a minor affair in itself, was to have an important effect on the general situation. When the two regiments moved out to their positions on December 19, one going east and the other going north, they could not initially form a common front. In theory they were joined somewhere along the railroad track below Lahez (11 miles south of Foy) but in fact there was a considerable gap between their closest elements. Each became so closely engaged in its local situation that the matter of contact was neglected. Colonel Sink was alarmed about the peril to his right flank from the beginning, but it was not until late on the night of December 19 that Colonel Ewell fully shared his apprehension.

Company A of the 501st was in reserve in a small wood just north of the quarry on the Neffe road, which made it the most rearward element in the 501st's general position. Several hundred yards to its rear were the guns of the 907th Glider Field Artillery Battalion's forward battery.

At 2300, December 19, a German patrol of thirty men came in between the company and the battery, moving from out of the northeast. A man on outpost duty for Company A saw the patrol and alerted the company. The patrol was permitted to come on. As it drew near the wood where the company had bivouacked, both the artillery and the infantry opened fire. The enemy dispersed into a nearby wood, though one member of the patrol was taken prisoner. Upon being interrogated he said that the patrol had come forward through the gap between the two infantry regiments and that its mission had been to get in behind and cut the Bastogne road. The incident gave the artillery grave fears about the security of their base and it also called Colonel Ewell's attention to the most vulnerable sector of his front.

Sometime on the morning of December 20, after the Germans had attacked at Bizory and then sideslipped northward, Company A of the 501st was attached to the 2d Battalion with the mission of occupying the woods south of the railroad and making contact with the 506th Parachute Infantry. However, it did not proceed immediately on this assignment and during most of that day the effort to join with the 506th was limited to patrol actions out of Company D, 501st, which was in reserve in the 2d Battalion. Four times during the day patrols from Company D tried to move north along the general line of the road running to Foy. But they were always turned back from the vicinity of Halt, where the enemy bad taken up fire positions.

At the same time Company D, 506th Parachute Infantry, was pushing rightward toward the railroad station at Halt against stubborn resistance. When evening of the 20th came the company had reached the Foy-Bizory road. It stayed there with its right flank some hundreds of yards distant from the railroad station at Halt, which was held by an enemy force. There had been no contact with the 501st. Colonel Sink, commander of the 506th, called both Headquarters, 501st Parachute Infantry, and Headquarters, 101st Division, and urged that the 501st swing leftward to meet him. He said that his force was standing on the railroad line which was supposed to be the regimental boundary - but this overstated the case.

The first three patrols which had gone out from Company D of the 501st to search for the 506th's flank had been turned back by fire from the Bois Jacques. They got no idea of the enemy strength in the forest area for they were beaten back by a scattering small-arms fire at long range whenever they moved to right of the Foy-Bizory road in an attempt to gain the railroad.

Corporal Frank Lasik of Company D, 501st, led out his fourth patrol of the day just as the evening twilight of the 20th came on. There were eight men with him, and instead of beating over the same ground as the earlier patrols they swung around to the westward of the Bizory-Foy road. When within a short distance of the railroad Lasik dropped six of his men and continued on with two others. They reached the rail line and moved east along it to within a hundred yards of the Halt station. At that point they saw a force of seven German tanks supported by a body of infantry moving straight toward them down the railroad track, and only 75 yards away. Private Manzi fired one shot toward the enemy force and then the three men withdrew as rapidly as they could. Lasik knew that Company A had been given an assignment and was supposed to be moving toward the same ground which the Germans were approaching. He rushed to the Battalion command post and told them to get word to Company A, 501st, that tanks were coming down the railway track.

Company A had moved out about 1600 on December 20 and was already engaged in clearing the woods that lay south of the railroad and west of the Foy-Bizory road. They found no enemy in the first wood and so they continued on to the next plantation lying south of the tracks and between them and the station at Halt. In the middle of this journey they met a patrol from the 506th Parachute Infantry. Until that meeting they had believed that the 506th was already on the railroad track. But from the patrol they learned that the actual flank of the 506th was about 600 yards north of the railroad track and that Company D, 506th, had been having a running fight with small groups of the enemy for control of the station at Halt.

From the second woods, Sergeant Lyle B. Chamberlain of Company A, 501st, was sent with a four-man patrol eastward along the tracks to search for the enemy. This was at just about the time that Lasik was getting back to warn the battalion. Sergeant Chamberlain's patrol moved through the swampy ground that lay to the left of the tracks and had gone but a short distance when they sighted a German patrol coming toward them. It looked to Chamberlain like the point of a company. Darkness was already closing around them and the German group did not see Sergeant Chamberlain's patrol. The patrol fell back on the company and reported what they had seen. Hastily, the 3d Platoon of Company A was deployed along the edge of the woods north of the railroad track to lay an ambush, for the enemy group which Sergeant Chamberlain had sighted was all northward of the track. While the platoon was deploying thick fog closed in around the woods and this coupled with the darkness reduced visibility to almost nothing. The Germans were allowed to approach within 10 to 15 yards before Company A opened fire. The surprise volley wholly disorganized the leading German platoon and the men who were not cut down ran to the rear to the swampy ground.

The whole Company A front had by this time become engaged. The enemy bad been advancing with two companies abreast astride the railway track. On Company A's right, the 1st and 2d Platoons did not get the same chance to close with the enemy at short range, and after the dispersion of the German right, mortar, grenade and automatic fire from the German force south of the tracks beat heavily against the two platoons. Because of the darkness and the fog the men of the company could get no idea what losses they were taking themselves and could only judge the progress of the action by the build-up of the enemy fire. They saw little or nothing of the Germans they were engaging. The skirmish went on with both forces firing toward the flashes and sounds in the position of the opposite force. Company A lost fifteen men in the night engagements, three of whom were killed in action. But in the black darkness the men of the Company thought at the time that they were taking much heavier losses. The fog made more vivid their impressions of the opposing fire while keeping them from feeling their own strength. The murk was so thick by this time that it was only by the sounds of fire that a man could tell where his nearest comrade was fighting.

While the fire fight on the south of the tracks continued, the Germans who had fallen back toward the swampy ground on the north of the track gradually collected themselves again. For half an hour or more there was a lull in the action on this side except that both forces tried to carry on at long range with hand grenades. Then the 3d Platoon of Company A heard the enemy moving out through the woods around their left flank.

Apprehensive that they would be outflanked if they maintained themselves in the forward ground, the 3d Platoon pulled back its own left flank to the westward so as to cover the rear of the company position. This change in the form of the enemy attack was also indicated on the right flank. Private First Class William C. Michel, a German-speaking soldier who was with the company executive officer, Lieutenant Joseph B. Schweiker, could hear the enemy shouting commands and telling his men to move out around the left and right of the American force. The order may have been a ruse intended to cover a withdrawal, but as the fire fight began to build up again it seemed to Lieutenant Schweiker that the enemy was actively pushing out around the flanks of Company A and threatening his rear.

At about 2230, December 20, Lieutenant Schweiker ordered the company to fall back to the line of the second woods. Lieutenant James C. Murphy called all of the squad leaders together and told them that the signal for withdrawal would be a long burst of machine-gun fire and that all of the other machine guns were to be kept quiet until this signal came. The withdrawal was made in reasonably good order, the circumstances considered.

When Company A took up its position in the second wood it was deployed to right of the railway line. The company was not pressed there at any time during the night. Apparently the Germans had ordered a withdrawal at about the same time. After staying in the woods for somewhat more than an hour the company withdrew a little to the southward and bivouacked in a third plantation.

The advance of the enemy down the railroad track had put them on the rear of Company D, 506th Parachute Infantry, but it was not until 0400 that Company D, which was somewhat engaged by small groups hitting directly at its front, discovered that its flank had been turned. Lieutenant Colonel Strayer reported to Colonel Sink that he believed an enemy force of about two platoons had penetrated between his battalion of the 506th and the 501st. But he did not know that Company D, 501st, was meeting this force frontally. Colonel Sink ordered Company D, 506th, to face some of its men toward the rear and bold their present ground. This, they did. The 1st Battalion, 506th, then in reserve at Luzery, was ordered to send Companies A and C forward to help contain the penetrating force. Both of these companies were badly depleted from their fight in Noville.

When morning of December 21 came the situation was about as follows: Company A, 501st, which had not been further disturbed during its bivouac, moved back up without opposition to exactly the same positions it bad occupied during the night engagement. Company D, 501st, which had bivouacked just to the south of Company A's bivouac area under the mistaken impression that it bad moved into the woods lying south of the railroad tracks, discovered its error when the light came. It immediately moved farther north, with one platoon going directly toward the objective woods and the others detouring east to clean out another small wood which they thought might contain enemy forces.

Through the accident of these shifts, the 501st Parachute Infantry thus had forces advancing from west, southwest and south as if to bring about a general envelopment of the German force at the Halt station. Coinciding with these movements from the south and west the two reserve companies (A and C) of the 506th reached the area to the northward at about 0815 and were committed in companies abreast to beat through the forests lying south and west of Company D's position. The morning of the 21st was heavy with fog; none of these approaching forces moving in on them from northeast, north, west, southwest and south was visible to the Germans dug in around the Halt station and in some of the plantations to westward of it. They were so completely misled as to their own position that when the platoons that had marched east for Company D, 501st, started their sweep north toward the Halt station, several of the enemy glimpsed them through the fog and came walking up to meet them, thinking they were friendly troops.

The line of the 506th came slowly but methodically on toward the railway tracks. Some of the Germans stayed to fight. Others gave up. Still others, in trying to get away were forced back into the killing ground established by the semicircular advance of the different forces of the 501st. By about 1100, December 2 1, the envelopment was complete and Companies A and C of the 506th had made full contact with units of the 501st along the railway line. The two companies were then ordered to return to Luzery, leaving Company D to solidify the front.

But in moving south and westward through the forest Companies A and C, 506th, discovered that the job was by no means completed. The morning advance had forced many of the enemy into the woods to the westward beyond the lines of Company A, 501st Parachute Infantry. The rat hunting continued throughout the day and it was almost dark before the 506th was convinced that the mop-up operation was complete. By that time it was realized that the original estimate of two platoons of enemy - these were troops of the 77th Volksgrenadier Regiment of the 26th Volksgrenadier Division - had far undershot the mark. The German force was more nearly the size of a battalion. About

100 of the enemy were captured and 55 killed by the units of the 506th Parachute Infantry in an operation that cost them only five or six casualties. About 80 Germans were driven into 501st's sector, where they were either killed or captured. Later, when the whole battle could be reviewed clearly, the senior commanders of 101st reckoned that the enemy missed his finest opportunity on this ground and during these hours. A strongly weighted attack straight down the railroad track could have carried through to Bastogne and turned the flanks of 501st and 506th Regiments.

[Because of the fog, this action was especially "confused" and neither regiment had any clear idea of what had happened or how the killing ground had been established. To clarify the story, Colonel Marshall held a series of company and patrol after-battle interviews. The story was put together with the aid mainly of the enlisted participants. This episode and the action at the Longvilly block were at first regarded as minor incidents in the general battle. As additional facts came to light - particularly the enemy story - their pivotal nature was revealed. General Higgins was of the opinion that had both regiments seen and exploited this opportunity more promptly and strongly, it would have produced one of the sharpest defeats to the enemy during the Bastogne battle. (Interview with Marshall February 5, 1946.)]

With the end of this engagement on December 21, re sectors of both the 501st and 506th became relatively quiet until after January 1. But there were other important consequences. Firm contact had been established between the two regiments, and it was never broken or weakened after that time the Germans were served notice that the road to Bastogne from the east and north was not open.

Out of these things also developed a new feeling of confidence among the artillery in the Bastogne area. They were now fully covered on the north and east by a reasonably strong shield and they could more easily direct their attention to the other parts of the defensive circle, wherever the danger mounted.

From December 21 on, the Germans gave over their attack against the 501st Parachute Infantry's part of the Bastogne front. The road to Bastogne did not lie through Colonel Ewell and his 501st.

11. RUNNING BATTLE

IN NOVILLE THEY were running short of armor-piercing shell as the morning of December 20 dawned. In Bastogne, General McAuliffe was wondering whether Noville was worth what he might have to pay to hold it, and was about to reach a decision. Deprived of any support from the commanding ridges, Noville is not a military position but just another village on low ground, and a perfect sinkhole for fog. The issue was already hanging in the balance because of the ammunition situation and the miscarriage of the American attack on December 19; only a little more pressure would tip it.

[The Historian had several discussions with Colonels Sink, Ewell, Kinnard and others concerning the nature of the Noville position at the time when the 101st Division attacked toward it in early January, and this was the estimate which all concerned placed upon it.]

On left flank of the 506th Parachute Infantry, the 502d had passed a quiet night. In midafternoon of December 19 the 502d had moved to Longchamps and established a perimeter defense there. Its 3d Battalion deployed on a high hill to south of the village. Its 1st Battalion was in the Bois de Niblamont which was southward of the hill. Initially, the 1st Battalion had held half of the front, but at 2400 of the 19th General McAuliffe told Lieutenant Colonel Steve Chappuis, commander of the 502d Parachute Infantry, that inasmuch as his regiment was the Division reserve he could leave one battalion on the northward-facing line. The 2d Battalion drew the assignment. It made no difference in any case, for though the battalion was stretched seven thousand yards, there was no action anywhere along its front that night.

But to the eastward where 506th stood guard, the boys who had prayed for morning soon wondered why. At 0730 two enemy tanks came hell-roaring through the field along the Houffalize road, swung in beside the first building of Noville, wheeled so as to protect each other and then stopped. On their way in they had knocked out a jeep with one shell, and had sprayed forward with their machine guns as they rushed. Unseeing, they came to a halt within ten yards of a bazooka team and the first rocket fired set one of the tanks on fire. Staff Sergeant Michael Lesniak, a tank commander, had heard the German armor roaring along. He dismounted from his tank, walked up the main street for a look, then went back and swung his gun in the right direction and moved to the center of the street. He fired before the enemy realized that he had gone into action and his first round finished the German tank. A third German tank that stayed just north along the road but out of sight in the fog threw a few loose shells into the town and one of them hit Sergeant Lesniak's tank, damaging the turret.

That was the beginning. Almost nothing that followed could be seen as clearly. During the next two hours the defensive perimeter was under constant attack from the German armor and infantry. But the enemy pressure developed quite unevenly as if their forces, too, were groping or were keeping active simply to conceal some larger design. It was battle with the bewildering shifts of a montage; there were momentary exposures and quick shiftings of scene. The enemy came on in groups of a few tanks supported by small parties of infantry and were held off by the armored infantry and paratroopers with their own weapons just long enough to let a friendly tank or tank destroyer get into firing position. Fog mixed with smoke from the burning buildings again mantled the country between the village and the ridges, diffusing the efforts of both forces. It was all but impossible for anyone to get any impression of how the tide was moving; the combatants could tell only what went on right before their eyes.

Curiously enough the tank destroyer men of 2d Platoon, Company C, 705th TD Battalion, who had taken position in the south of Noville, had the impression that in these early morning hours the infantry was standing off a full-fledged attack. They could see only a hundred yards beyond their own guns and they could hear large numbers of enemy tracked vehicles moving toward them through the fog. Their imaginings were further stimulated by a direct hit on one tank destroyer at the outset which killed the gunner, Corporal Stephen Cook, and wounded several of the crew. For two hours they fired in the general direction of where they thought the German armor was massing; they could see no targets but they thought their unobserved fire might have some deterring effect. At 1000, December 20, the fog quite suddenly lifted and the sky became almost clear. In the field within view of the tank destroyer force were 15 German tanks; they were proceeding toward their own lines at about 1,000 yards range. Four of the tanks were hit and disabled and the tank destroyer men were confident that their own shells did it. They had seen their shots hit home and watched Private Steve E. Reed empty seven boxes of caliber .50 ammunition into the German crews as they tried to flee across the fields.

Just before the fog had cleared a Tiger tank had charged right into the heart of Noville. Visibility among the buildings was just about zero. The tank stopped in front of the command post of Company B, 20th Armored Infantry Battalion. The tanker swung his gun uncertainly toward the door. Captain Omar Billett said a quick prayer. A joker beside him remarked, "Don't look now, but there is an 88 pointing at you."

[Harwick witnessed this incident and gave this detail during his informal interview with Colonel Marshall which was not committed to writing.]

Sergeant Lesniak's tank was within twenty yards but the German had failed to see him in the fog; by rotating his damaged turret just a short space to the right Lesniak had his gun dead on the Tiger. At twenty yards he fired three rounds of 75mm. at the German tank without doing any apparent damage. The German quickly put his tank into reverse. But the left track ran up and over a jeep. The jeep was completely crushed but at the same time it fouled the track and beached the tank. The German kept on pushing back-the jeep under him. He next collided with a half-track and the tank tipped dangerously over on its right side.

[Confirmed by Harwick's description to Marshall though Harwick also thought that a tank destroyer came from the other direction and fired on the German tanks. In this he appears to have been mistaken.]

That was enough for the German crew. They jumped from the tank and ran out of the town, going through the American lines without getting a shot fired at them, such was the thickness of the fog.

The radio inside the Tiger was on a busy channel, and talk flowed on inside the dead tank. It looked like a wide-open opportunity, but before the command post could round up anyone who could understand German, the channel went out. The tankers destroyed this Tiger with thermite and later on they caught hell from Colonel Roberts for not bringing the tank back to Bastogne.

[Colonel Roberts told Westover about this but Westover did not make note of it at the time.]

But they had a good excuse. The losses among the tank drivers were already such that they did not have enough men to maneuver their own armor. Two tanks were without drivers and partly without crews. So the tankers asked the paratroopers if there were any men among them who could handle tanks and two of Major Harwick's men of the 1st Battalion, 506th Parachute Infantry, climbed aboard and started out with the Shermans. Later on both men were killed in their tanks during the withdrawal.

[Harwick reported this to Colonel Marshall and at the same

time he was telling Colonel Sink about it and was expressing his regrets that he had lost some good men. He even named the men. However, the tankers did not report to Westover that they used any paratroopers at this time, and therefore the facts are not confirmed by the armored units. It is notable all the way through these reports that both forces minimize the help received from the other group. Often that is not an oversight on their part; they simply lacked the information.]

They knew now that they would not be able to hold Noville much longer. The clearing of the fog revealed to Major Hustead (now commanding the 20th Armored Infantry Battalion) and his staff a situation they had already suspected. During the night of the 19th the men on the outposts had heard enemy armor moving across their rear, particularly to the southwestward.

[Members of the armored units reported these impressions to Westover but he did not write them down in his report.]

In the morning, patrols had gone out, and although they couldn't tell much because of the enveloping fog, they found enough to confirm the fact that enemy forces were between them and Bastogne. Hustead had lost radio contact with Combat Command B Headquarters during the night. So in the morning he sent First Lieutenant Herman C. Jacobs to Foy; he was to get to Headquarters, 3d Battalion, 506th Parachute Infantry, in Foy and use their radio to inform Combat Command B of the situation and request that the Noville garrison either be withdrawn or reinforced. He carried out the mission in a half-track and several times on the way to Foy he blundered into enemy parties and had to shoot his way through. But at Foy he found no one; by this time 3d Battalion was engaging the enemy to the south of the village. Lieutenant Jacobs continued on to Bastogne and found Colonel Roberts who sent his only available reserve - an antiaircraft platoon - forward. But the platoon was blocked by enemy forces before it could get to Foy. The Germans were coming across the road from both sides. When the fog rolled away the men in Noville could look southward and see the circling armor. To make their isolation more complete, they bad lost all contact with the main body of 506th Parachute Infantry and they did not know whether the situation at Foy was developing for or against them.

The Germans had already made their onfall against Colonel Sink's support position. In early morning, December 20, the 3d Battalion of the 506th received light shelling and flat-trajectory fire along its lines at Foy. During the night and through the first hours of daylight the enemy had taken advantage of the heavy fog and moved in very close to the American outposts, though it seems probable that they knew very little about the location of the American lines and were only groping.

At 0800, December 20, a force of about two companies of infantry supported by three tanks attacked toward the ground defended by Companies I and H. By 0900, they had driven in far enough to put direct fire on the American positions with their supporting weapons. The tank destroyers of 3d Platoon, Reconnaissance Company of the 705th Tank Destroyer Battalion were not in position to give the infantry any direct fire support during the engagement. They were in the woods south of Foy when the attack came on, and in the later stages of the action they were established as roadblocks, but during that morning they did not fire on any enemy armor. Company G in Recogne was engaged by another company of German infantry supported by three tanks. The command post of the 3d Battalion in Foy came under direct fire from an enemy tank. Until 1030 the Battalion held its ground in Foy and then withdrew to the high ground south of the village. Here it reformed for the counterattack.

It was about mid-morning when 101st Airborne Division Headquarters called the 502d Parachute Infantry and directed that its 3d Battalion (under Lieutenant Colonel John P. Stopka) attack through Recogne and gain contact with the American

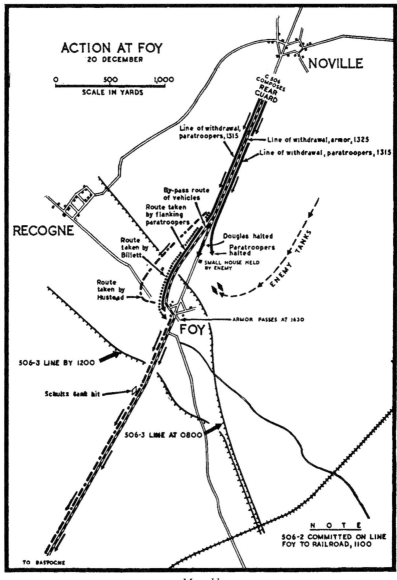

Map 11

force at Noville, thus reestablishing the left flank. The battalion crossed the line of departure at 1130 and then pushed right on, meeting little opposition.

But when the 3d Battalion, 502d, reached Recogne a change in the order came. At somewhere around noon General McAuliffe had decided that Noville wasn't important enough to warrant a last-ditch stand on the inferior ground around the village. Colonel Stopka was accordingly instructed to make a limited attack forward to cover the extrication of Major Harwick's men of the 3d Battalion, 506th. That battalion was to fight the same kind of action on the other flank. It was figured that the Noville force could sideslip into the area of the 502d once Stopka's battalion got up to it. However, his Battalion had fought its way only a short distance past Recogne when the plan was again changed.

Colonel Sink, commanding the 506th, had looked the situation over and decided that the best way out was for Major Harwick's force to retire down the Bastogne road. Colonel Stopka's battalion remained in position on a line running through Recogne with its left flank extended westward to join the 2d Battalion of the 502d. Its advance had been made wholly without artillery support because of the dense fog.

Radio communication between Bastogne and Noville was not reestablished until 1300. The order then came through on the artillery radio net to Harwick and Hustead that their command would withdraw to the Bastogne perimeter of defense. They were told that an attack on Foy was being made immediately to relieve the pressure on Noville. When they saw that the attention of the enemy was diverted to the Foy attack, they were to make a break for the south.

A few local problems had to be solved in Noville preceding the withdrawal. A considerable amount of ammunition had to be destroyed. There were more than fifty wounded men awaiting evacuation. But the shrinkage of manpower in the Noville force through battlefield deaths and casualties already evacuated had totalled so many men that, despite a steady loss in vehicles, there were enough tanks, half-tracks and trucks left to move back all the casualties and permit all the armored units and most of the paratroopers to ride out of Noville.

Company C of the 506th was already south of Noville in a

reserve position, and accordingly, it was nominated as the advance guard to move out on foot. Three tanks would support Company C. The half-tracks and jeeps loaded with the wounded would come next in the column. Then would follow the main body, the personnel carriers and armor. Those of the infantry who couldn't find a ride would move out in file on both sides of the road. Company B of the 506th was to be the rear guard, supported by four tank destroyers. One platoon from that company was detailed to destroy everything useful that could not be evacuated.

At 1315, December 20, Company C took off. At 1325 the first vehicles quit Noville.33 Major Hustead and his engineer officer had prepared the ammunition dump for demolition; the dump was alongside a building and they were hopeful that the blast would lay the building low and block the highway. Hustead waited until the last vehicle had passed the ammunition point. He then gave the engineer the signal to set off the delayed charge. They heard the explosion as they moved on down the road.

The start was good. Until 1300 the air had been crystal clear for most of the noon hour. Then, as if Providence again chose to intervene in their favor, the fog closed around them and screened their departure from the enemy. They knew that they could be, heard and they wondered whether the Germans would try to take them in flank while they were on the move. But the fire which might have been turned against the road was spared them and they moved along quite easily, except for an occasional flurry of bullets.

A little protecting belt of armor - one armored M8, followed by four half-tracks, and five medium tanks - moved in front of the vehicles containing the wounded. Just beyond the village, one of the tanks broke down and bad to be destroyed with thermite. The armored car took off at full speed without waiting for the others, and got to Bastogne without receiving any fire.

The column continued on toward Foy and the half-tracks had come abreast of a farmhouse within 500 yards of the village when occurred one of those chance things which may change the whole course of a battle despite their own intrinsic unimportance.

In the leading half-track the shutter dropped and the driver could not see. The driver raised up and moved his arm to adjust the shutter and Major James B. Duncan mistook the gesture and thought that the man bad been wounded and was holding his eyes. So Duncan quickly pulled the hand brake. That stopped the entire column. The first half-track was rammed from behind by the second half-track which had lost its brakes. The third half-track pulled up close. At that moment bullets and grenades bit into the column from both sides of the road. The men could not see clearly what they were fighting but they knew that some Germans were deployed in the ditches and that they were also drawing fire from the house. Major Duncan figured that he had to fight it out on that ground. The machine gunners in the half-tracks put heavy fire on the ditches; and the dismounted riflemen, after flattening themselves, blazed away with their tommy guns. In ten minutes the skirmish was over. Some of the enemy had been cut down. Others had dispersed into the fog.

[The S57 report of this whole episode is vague and confused. It is to be noted that both the infantry and the tank destroyer units reported that there was a German roadblock at Foy and that this was what checked the column. These forces were not up front and were not in position to see. The assumption was a natural one in view of the circumstances.]

The fourth half-track had withdrawn a short distance to keep from jamming the column. Major Duncan had gone back that way. The amount of firing that he could hear from forward among the half-tracks, mingled with the noise of the firing of the 3d Battalion, 506th, which was attacking north toward Foy, gave Duncan an exaggerated idea of the importance of the action. He asked for the tanks to get forward and fire on the house.

Meanwhile the three half-tracks had shoved on. Back through the column all men had dismounted and taken to the ditches. Major Hustead came for-ward to see what was blocking the road and he met Major Duncan near the head of the column. Both officers then tried to get the tanks moving again. The crew of the first tank told Major Hustead they had no ammunition. The second tank couldn't fire either; there was no ammunition for the big gun and the machine gun was jammed. Duncan prodded two of the tanks into carrying out the order and they shelled the house until it caught fire. Thereupon, they backed away. Duncan was still worrying because be could bear small-arms fire, so he ordered them to go in. As they moved away they were caught broadside by fire from three German tanks which had slipped through the fog from the eastward. The first American tank caught fire. In the second American tank the driver was hit and the tank came to a halt.

Because of the murk, men who were only a few yards back in the column could get no true idea of what was happening. Captain William G. Schultz, the tank commander, was in the fifth tank. He walked up to the third tank, which was short of personnel, and drove it on down the road past the two disabled tanks. They were beyond his help and he thought that if he kept moving the rest of the column would follow.

But in this he was mistaken. He drove through Foy alone and about a quarter-mile beyond the village his tank was hit by a shell from an enemy tank and disabled, but Captain Schultz and his men got out alive and walked on into Bastogne. Meanwhile, Major Hustead and Captain Billett were striving to get the column moving. A tank destroyer of the 705th TD Battalion whipped up from the rear of the column to try to get a line on the yet unseen German tanks. A Sherman tank from the forward group backed straight toward the tank destroyer and the tank destroyer, reversing direction to save itself, backed over and crushed a jeep.

[Duncan was not in the jeep at the time and no one was injured.]

Then the Sherman moved on up to have another go at the house and it was hit by a shell from a German tank and exploded in flames. The turret blew off into the road and blocked the passage. The driver of the fifth tank, who had been with Schultz, had moved up and taken over the second tank just before it was demolished. This left the fifth tank driverless. As the road was now blocked by the turret, Hustead and Billett moved back and forth among the tankers looking for a driver so they could start the column moving across the field to Foy. There was not a single response. Every tanker replied that he was qualified for some other kind of work but couldn't move a tank. The paratroopers and the armored infantry jumped to the conclusion that the men were dogging it. They walked among the tankers cursing them and calling them "yellow bastards"; they threatened *[sic]* to beat up one man whom they suspected of being a driver. But they were all wrong about it. Most of these men were new replacements. Some were cooks, some were mechanics and some were riflemen. They were tankers only in that they belonged to a tank organization. The impasse at Foy could only be charged to the replacement system.

The paratroopers farther back along the road had picked themselves up and moved out through the fields on both sides. The group on the right swept all the way to Foy, met no organized resistance but bagged a few Germans whom they found wandering around in the fog. The tank destroyer force at the rear also became restive and at 1430 First Lieutenant Tom E. Toms led his vehicles down a little stream line on the right of the road and by way of this defilade entered Foy from the west. He had gotten there in ten minutes. The paratroopers who had swung out to the right reached the village at the same time. The tank destroyers were not quite through for the day.

The foot troops who had swung out to the east of the road were stopped by the line of fire which the unseen German tanks were throwing at the Shermans at the front of the column. They sent word back to the main body. However, the danger was removed by help from an unexpected quarter. Private First Class Thomas E. Gallagher was driving one of the tank destroyers which had gone into Foy and was on his way to an assembly area in a woods south of the village when be was stopped by an officer of the 3d Battalion, 506th Parachute Infantry. He knew the location of the German tanks and told Gallagher to go after them. Gallagher said he had no crew and no one to work the gun. Two paratroopers climbed into the tank destroyer and took over the gun. Gallagher then moved forward and with the infantrymen doing the firing the tank destroyer engaged one tank at 200 yards range and destroyed it. The other German tank escaped over the hill.

Because of the fog Major Hustead and Captain Billett hadn't seen the infantry parties move out to right and left. Billett felt that he ought to clear a route for the tanks and vehicles to advance and he sent back for his outfit, Company B of the 20th Armored Infantry Battalion. One platoon stayed back in the column with the vehicles and he started out with the other two platoons moving through the fields to the right. Major Hustead had the same idea but didn't know that it had already been put into execution twice on this same flank. He gathered about 20 paratroopers together and made an additional hook to the right. The odd part of it was that although this party groped its way forward over the same ground as the others, they did so in time to reap part of the harvest. The enemy groups around Foy were now feeling the heat from both directions. Hustead's sweep toward Foy resulted in the capture of 43 Germans.

In the village Hustead met troops of the 3d Battalion, 506th, who had advanced from the south and he asked them, "Has our armor come through?"

The men had seen the three half-tracks and Captain Schultz's tank go by and they thought this was the armor Major Hustead was talking about. So they reassured him. Hustead borrowed a jeep and drove to Bastogne to report to Colonel Roberts that he had completed his mission. But when he got to town be learned that he was mistaken and could only tell Colonel Roberts that the column was on its way and should soon arrive.

Major Hustead in Bastogne and Captain Billett in Foy were both on the radio urging the column to come around to the right. But Major Duncan and Second Lieutenant Burleigh P. Oxford were already jockeying the column through the fields. The fifth tank was on its way. A crew of paratroopers had climbed aboard after telling the tankers, "We'll learn bow to run the son of a bitch." When the column drew into Foy some of the vehicles got stuck in the soft ground. Lieutenant Oxford dismounted all of the men and got the winches and the manpower working first of all on extricating the vehicles that contained the wounded. At dusk of December 20 the column was finding its way through Foy and past the lines of the 3d Battalion, 506th. The command in Bastogne had intended that the force would go into a defensive position on the high ground south of Foy. But Hustead told Colonel Roberts that the column was dead beat and bad better be brought into Bastogne. The tank destroyers under Lieutenant Toms stayed in Foy supporting the 3d Battalion.

Team Desobry had gone to Noville with fifteen tanks; it limped back with only four. The 1st Battalion of the 506th Parachute Infantry was in full strength when it went to Team Desobry's support. It lost 13 officers and 199 enlisted men at Noville.61 By their combined efforts they bad destroyed or badly crippled somewhere between twenty and thirty known enemy tanks of all types including not less than three Mark VIs.

[Members of the armored units put a lower estimate on the damage done to enemy armor than the paratroopers did and the

figures given here are a compromise of the two. It is obvious that the battle was such that an accurate count could not be made.]

They probably damaged or destroyed many more. Headquarters of the 506th estimated that the assaults of the German infantry had cost the enemy the equivalent of half a regiment.

[As to the identification of enemy units in the Neville action, the G-2 report shows that by the night of December 20 six prisoners captured in the Foy-Recogne area had been identified as coming from 2d Panzer Division.]

Yet all of these material measurements of what had been achieved were mean and meager weighed against the fact that the men of Noville had held their ground for a decisive 48 hours during which time the defense of Bastogne had opportunity to organize and grow confident of its own strength.

12. FIRST ACTION AT MARVIE

AT 0645 ON DECEMBER 20, the enemy shelled Team O'Hara's roadblock on the Wiltz-Bastogne road about 1,300 yards east of Marvie. The fog was thick and little could be seen of the enemy's movements out along the road. But as the light grew, the tankers could hear enemy armor moving somewhere in the fog up beyond the block. At around 0900 the fog lifted a little and they saw a dozen German soldiers trying to break up the block. A concentration from the 420th Field Artillery Battalion caught this group while they were, tugging away at the felled logs. Two were killed (they were later identified as part of an engineer working party) and the others fled the fire. The enemy then put smoke on the roadblock - enough to conceal the block and the terrain right around it. Figuring that an infantry attack might be coming, Team O'Hara covered the block with fire from mortars and assault guns. It is believed that this fire fended off the thrust toward Colonel

The village of Marvie, looking north.

Men waiting in the regimental command post of the 327th Glider Infantry.

O'Hara's front and deflected it toward Marvie, where five of O'Hara's light tanks had taken up position the night before.

In the meantime Colonel Joseph H. Harper, commanding the 327th Glider Infantry, had been getting acquainted with Colonel O'Hara. The 327th had taken over the command post at Mande-St.-Étienne at 1500 on December 19, and at 1630 its 1st Battalion had been attached to Colonel Ewell's 501st Parachute Infantry to support his right flank. At 0400 on the 20th the 327th command post and the 2d Battalion of that regiment were ordered into Bastogne and at 0600 they marched on into the town. Without a pause, the 2d Battalion, 327th, moved straight on to Marvie and took over that village from the 326th Engineers. The 3d Battalion remained in Flamizoulle (some 2,000 yards east of Flamierge) and established its command post in the woods at (494610).

The 2d Battalion entered Marvie just about as the enemy first opened fire on Team O'Hara's roadblock. *[This entry was made between 0630 and 0700.]*

Colonel Harper had been told by Division that the reconnaissance group of light tanks would be in support of his 2d Battalion. Going straight away to see Colonel O'Hara, he said to him, "I've been told to hold this sector. I understand from Division that you are in support of me and I would like to go on

139

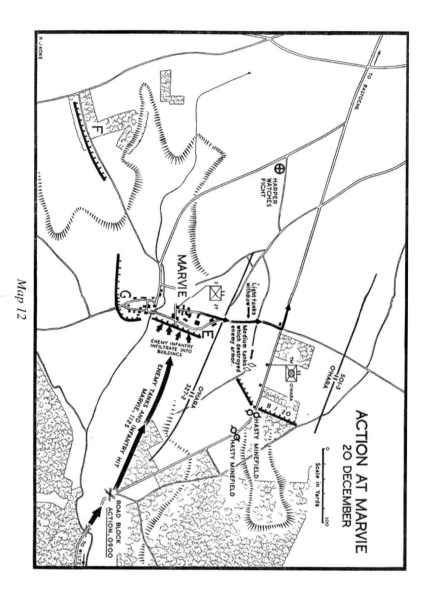

Map 12

a reconnaissance."

O'Hara said, "Let's get started." With them when they went out was Lieutenant Colonel Roy L. Inman, commanding the 2d Battalion, 327th Glider Infantry. The officers discussed the relationship of their respective forces as they made the reconnaissance. Under the existing arrangement, Colonel O'Hara's force was not under Colonel Harper's command, for the armored force was still not attached to the 101st Division but was in support only. Colonel Inman had moved his 2d Battalion, 327th, in on the right flank of Colonel O'Hara's force with his line so extended as to secure the village and then bending southwestward to the main road just above Remoifosse. This was a distance of about 2,500 yards. The Engineers had three outposts distributed over this southeastern facing arc and none of them had as yet been engaged. It was agreed that Colonel O'Hara would be responsible for the defense of his immediate front and that Colonel Inman, who would take over from the Engineers immediately, would be responsible for the sector to right of O'Hara's. Harper then left Inman and drove down the main road toward Remoifosse. He established the southwestward extension of his line on the forward slope of the hill over which the main road passes a little more than half way from Bastogne to Remoifosse. The position thus chosen was a few hundred yards north of where the original Engineer outpost bad been.

After looking over the situation and making sure that his men were where he wanted them, Colonel Harper drove back to Marvie. The jeep reached the road intersection just west of Marvie. There Harper stopped for a moment and debated with himself whether to go on into the village or take the west-running road and have a quick look at the high ground above the village. He decided in favor of taking a look and the jeep moved on up the hill.

At 1125, December 20, Colonel Inman's command post in

Marvie (2d Battalion, 327th Glider Infantry) reported to Colonel O'Hara that they were receiving a great deal of shelling and that they could see enemy tanks coming toward them.

[Made from Colonel O'Hara's journal. There was no time entry in the 327th Glider Infantry journal covering this incident. Colonel Harper, commander of the 327th, had the impression that it occurred much earlier in the morning.]

This movement had already been observed from within O'Hara's sector. Yet Harper, driving up the hill at the very moment of the attack, was unaware that anything untoward was breaking until he got to the crest of the hill. There he turned about and saw the enemy guns blazing from the edge of the woods directly southeast of Marvie and their point-blank fire hitting among the houses of the village.

Harper could see that the fire came from tanks within the wood but he could not be certain how many. The barrage was followed immediately by an advance out of the woods by four enemy tanks and six half-tracks. They were well spread out and they advanced slowly, firing as they came, apparently drawn on by the prospect of an easy success over the light tanks. These tanks kept dodging in and out among the buildings and the enemy fire appeared to follow their movements closely. The light tanks replied futilely with their 37mm. guns and the enemy armor appeared to come on more boldly. Feeling that the presence of his unit, rather than helping Colonel Inman's men, was drawing more high-velocity fire into the town, the light tank commander asked Colonel O'Hara for permission to withdraw. It was granted. By then, one of the light tanks had been set afire by a shell burst; a second had been hit in the suspension system but could make its escape by backing up the hill.

Yet Colonel Harper did not know all of these things. He saw the tanks quit the village and concluded that they had been routed and were deserting his infantry.

Up on the hill behind Marvie, Colonel O'Hara's larger guns

kept silent. In front of the oncoming armor a German self-propelled 75mm. gun was pacing the advance. Its gunner spotted a half-track near O'Hara's command post and fired several quick rounds at it. The shells hit an Engineer jeep, demolished a one-ton trailer and blew through the lower portion of the command post, killing a cow. The command post was in the first floor of the house and this fire was hitting into the basement right under the headquarters.

The tanks were by now almost broadside to Team O'Hara at 700 yards range. Firing at right angles to their own front, two of Team O'Hara's medium tanks opened up on the line of Mark IVs and half-tracks. The Germans never saw what hit them for they were still shooting at the light tanks now pulling out through the end of the village. One Mark IV was blown up by a direct hit from one of the mediums. The other Sherman knocked out a second Mark IV and one of the half-tracks, the fire killing all of the tank crew and most of the men in the personnel carrier. One German tank fled to the rear. The fourth tank dashed for Marvie where the infantry destroyed it with bazooka fire. The self-propelled gun, having gotten almost into the village before the Sherman opened fire, tried to turn about. It was hit from all sides and it went up like a torch.

In the last stage of the German advance, the half-tracks had sped forward and increased their interval so that they were almost closing on the first houses when the tank line was destroyed. They kept going. They got to the streets of the village and the infantry jumped down. With one small exception the glider troops stayed right where they were and met the German on-fall without flinching. The attack had come just as the relief of the Engineer units had been completed, and some of the Engineers were moving out of the north end of Marvie. Men from Inman's heavy mortar section, stationed in an apple orchard, saw the Engineer party leave as the fire began. They could not understand what the movement of troops was about and they thought that part of their own Battalion was withdrawing. And so they followed.

Colonel Harper, watching all of these things from the hill, made the same mistake as his mortar section. He thought that his men had been stampeded and that the village was gone. He called General McAuliffe on the radio, told him what he bad seen and said that he was on his way to gather the men and that he would make a counterattack. His car sped back over the route it had come and Harper started to rally his men. Then he learned that most of the party were Engineers and that only the mortar squad from among his command had displaced. He told that squad to get back into the battle and they moved at once. This error in judgment is the only instance during the siege of Bastogne when any American Infantryman is known to have left his position under fire and without orders.

Colonel Harper, still outside the village, called Colonel Inman on his radio. The executive officer of the 2d Battalion, 327th Glider Infantry, Major R. B. Galbreaith, answered the call. He said that both Colonel Inman and Captain Hugh Evans, commanding officer of Company G, which was holding the village, had been hit by a tank shell while making a reconnaissance just as the German onslaught began. He did not know how badly they were wounded. Harper asked him, "Are you still in the village?"

"Yes," Galbreaith answered. "Yes, but the Germans are here also. We expect to drive them out."

The close-in fighting continued into the early afternoon. Inman's men stayed in their foxholes. Some died there, shot at ten yards' range by machine guns as they tried to stop the half-tracks with their rifle and tommy gun fire, their bodies almost cut in half where the machine guns had ripped them through. Their comrades found them later sitting stiffly at their weapons. Colonel Harper himself inspected these positions. He noted that every one of his dead was still facing forward as if trying to engage the enemy. The bazooka men bad likewise met the attack head-on. Some of the German infantry, clearing away from the half-tracks, had ducked into the houses. The glider men went in after them and cleaned them out house by house. Within two hours twenty Germans were prisoners and thirty were dead in Marvie. First Lieutenant Stanley A. Morrison of Company G, who had been captured when the Germans first came into the village, was recaptured by his own men. Colonel Inman bad lost five men killed, each of them killed in a foxhole while resisting the half-tracks. Fifteen men of Company G were wounded in the action.

During all that time, Team O'Hara sat high and dry on the ridge, taking no part in the engagement except during the brief gun duel. On the right flank that force received some small-arms fire but the enemy made no attempt to close on that side and the armored infantry in Team O'Hara's position was too far away to lend any support to the men in Marvie. That village was again clear by about 1300. At 1400 some of Colonel O'Hara's tankers saw an enemy half-track stuck in the mud about 150 yards southeast of Marvie. It had been with the striking force during the morning and had become bogged. In the previous excitement all hands had overlooked it. The tankers quickly knocked it out.

At 1420, December 20, the enemy put smoke on Marvie. Some of the tanks made another sally from the woods but changed their minds. The situation began to ease and Colonel Inman's men went about improving their positions, digging their foxholes narrow and very deep and right next to the foundations of the houses. The day ended fairly quietly but with a definite change in the weather. The Ardennes was cold and frozen. The ground had hardened enough for the tracked vehicles to get about over the hills in almost any direction. Still no snow bad fallen.

Now, as the first skirmish ended around Marvie, the first flurries fell. Soon the ridges were whitening and the snows thickened during the next few days. Increasing cold, light winds and deep drifts changed many of the characteristics of the battle. One of the problems that now pressed most heavily on the commanders was to get their men indoors and keep them from freezing. Villages became places of refuge not only from enemy fire but from the cold. The Belgian villagers, clinging stubbornly to their homes even in the face of the German attack, had to be evacuated to provide shelter and cover for the infantry. In a world of white, the forest plantations were the only other areas of easy concealment for troops. The local actions swirled more and more around these two objectives - to capture a few houses or to take a line of fir trees.

13. THE RESPITE

ON DECEMBER 21 and 22 the opposing forces around the northeast sector simply sparred with one another. *[This is perhaps an over-simplification. There were fairly heavy attacks against the north on December 21 and one running engagement in the southwest, but the failure of the enemy to press a general attack against the Bastogne defenses during the two days is conspicuous.]*

The enemy had been stopped cold at Neffe and Mont by Colonel Ewell's 501st Parachute Infantry and supporting units. The effort to slip through the ground held by the forces of Colonels O'Hara and Harper had been equally unsuccessful though less costly. After these futile passes, and following the shock action at Noville, the enemy seemed almost to abandon the effort to break through Bastogne and concerned himself with extending the westward flow of his forces on both sides of it so as to complete the encirclement.

The road to Neufchâteau was cut by the Germans on the night of December 20, isolating Bastogne. General McAuliffe had gone that way just a few hours before to talk to the Corps commander.

[The precise hours of the cutting of the Neufchâteau road is not known and the statement on which this paragraph is based is taken from the interview with General McAuliffe.]

It was a pregnant conversation. General McAuliffe said that he was certain he could hold on for at least 48 hours and maybe longer. General Middleton replied that in view of the fact that the hour would probably come when communications could not be maintained, General McAuliffe would have to be prepared to act on his own. He pointed out that the 116th Panzer Division was coming in on General McAuliffe's flank - in addition to the three German divisions already fighting him. McAuliffe said, "I think we can take care of them." Middleton said that he certainly wanted to hold Bastogne but was not sure that it could be done in view of recent developments. It was important, General Middleton added, that the road to the southwestward be kept open as long as possible.

As General McAuliffe walked out the door, Middleton's last comment was: "Now, don't get yourself surrounded." McAuliffe noticed that he said it very lightly and felt that the Corps commander was simply having a little joke in a tense moment.

[Quoted directly. According to an interview with Colonel Walter C. Stanton, Deputy Chief of Staff, VIII Corps, General Middleton never weakened in his desire to hold Bastogne. On the 19th, however, Lieutenant General George S. Patton, Jr., commanding general, Third Army, ordered a withdrawal. Colonel Stanton believed this order was possibly influenced by the weak showing of First Army. The VIII Corps order appeared on December 20. Interview by Captain L. B. Clark, 3d Information and Historical Service, and Captain K. W. Hechler, 2d Information and Historical Service, January 16, 1945, vicinity Assenois, Belgium.]

General McAuliffe went on out, jumped in his car and told the driver to make for Bastogne as fast as he could get there. He figured he was already surrounded - or just about so. A half hour after he did come over the road, it was cut by the German armor.

That was not, however, an unmixed evil, for it brought an important change in the relationship of the forces in the defense. During its first two days the infantry and the armor had collaborated well but they had not been a team. On the first night, General McAuliffe had asked that the armor (Combat Command B, 10th Armored Division) be attached to him and its commander Colonel Roberts had said, "What do you know about armor?"

General McAuliffe had replied, "Maybe you want the 101st Division attached to your Combat Command."

[Confirmed by other members of the staff who were present. This exchange of words, however, does not appear in the Westover interview with Colonel Roberts.]

It was partly because of this division in the command authority, and partly because the armor and the infantry were units strange and new to each other, that during the first stage there was a lack of cohesion." That lack was felt more as a moral than as a tactical thing. To one staff officer of the Division the armor along the front seemed "like a will o' the wisp."

The armor felt the same way about the infantry. Each force had the feeling those first few days that it was propping up the front pretty much unhelped. In general, neither force was feeling the presence of the other strongly nor having a clear idea bow much support was being received from it. Liaison was fragmentary. Both tankers and infantrymen had bad to come out of their comers fighting and during the first crucial hours they had no choice but to look straight ahead and slug.

But with the cutting of the Neufchâteau road and the isolating of the Bastogne garrison, General Middleton called General McAuliffe and told him that the armor (Combat Command B) and all other troops within the circle were now under his command.

General Middleton also called Colonel Roberts and told him, "Your work has been quite satisfactory but I have so many divisions that I can't take the time to study two sets of reports from the same area." Colonel Roberts reported in person to General McAuliffe to do command liaison and from that time on until the siege was lifted his post was almost exclusively at the 101st Division command post. The result was that the coordination was complete. Roberts, a veteran tank commander, was particularly concerned that the armor be used properly, used to the maximum effect and not wasted. He strongly resisted the attempts of infantry commanders to use tanks as roadblocks. He worked specifically to get his armor quickly released after each engagement so that there would always be a maximum strength in General McAuliffe's mobile reserve for the next emergency. In the middle of the siege he published a mimeographed memorandum to the infantry officers on the right ways to use tanks.

The order to Combat Command B on December 21 from VIII Corps to "hold the Bastogne line at all costs" gives a key to General Middleton's view of the situation during this period. On the evening before, he had talked with McAuliffe and bad expressed a doubt whether the strength at Bastogne was sufficient for the task. All along he bad been willing to make the gamble of an encircled force at Bastogne, and for a few hours he may have felt that the gamble was dubious. Now be had come to believe the gamble would succeed and that the battle must be fought out on that line. There was no longer any doubt or question anywhere in the camp. From this hour the action of all concerned, the VIII Corps commander, the 101st Division commander, and the armored force commander of Combat Command B-Middleton, McAuliffe, and Roberts-became wholly consistent with the resolve that Bastogne could and would be held.

[This conclusion is supported by the proof that air resupply of the Bastogne position immediately became a foremost concern of VIII Corps, and that VIII Corps Headquarters labored throughout December 21 to make the operation possible.]

General McAuliffe now had the answer to all of his questions. No situation could have been more clearly defined. During the first two days he had entertained many doubts and bad continued to wonder just what the situation was. He had heard about various groups from the 28th and 106th Divisions which were still out fighting somewhere and might fall back upon him. The 7th Armored Division was supposed to be somewhere up around

Security guard of the 101st Airborne Division near the 502d Parachute Infantry Command Post.

St. Vith. He had also had to worry about the organization of stragglers. At the first, part of the 28th Division had been screening him on the south flank. Its commander, Major General Norman D. Cota, had called him on the morning of December 20 and said, "I'd like to see you," and McAuliffe had replied, "I'm too damned busy." Cota then said, "I'll come up to see you."

Now, on the 21st, McAuliffe knew that General Cota would not be coming to see him, and that the only situation involving American troops about which he would have to worry for a while was the situation right within the two-and-one-half mile circle of German forces closed around Bastogne. The only support he could expect for the time being was just what he had - all within ranging distance of his own 105mm. Batteries. It was a nice, clear-cut position and it had materialized in just about the way that he had expected upon first reaching Bastogne. *[General McAuliffe says specifically that from the moment he reached Bastogne he expected to get cut off because there seemed to be nothing in front of him that would prevent it.]*

But what he had not foreseen, something that came like a gift form the gods, was that after the first hard collision, the enemy would give him a comparative respite in which to reflect on his situation and knit his armor and infantry close together, now that both were his to work with as he saw fit. The Germans had spent two days trying to break on through Bastogne. They had failed to crush it; they would try to choke it. But while they were building up around the west and south, the pressure against the city relaxed. *[It is notable that December 22 was the least active day on the Bastogne front.]*

The flow of bubbles on the G-2 overlays, showing the extension of the enemy to the south and westward, was moving along. Panzer Lehr Division had been the first to break upon the Bastogne rock. But the 26th Volksgrenadier Division had also come in from the east. A captured map showed that it had failed in one of its appointments, for the 26th Volksgrenadier was to have had the honor of capturing Bastogne.

The Germans were traveling light. Their commanders had told them that Bastogne was bursting with American food and that they could eat when they got there. Some had gone hungry for three days while trying to reach the American rations. Too, the enemy fire power manifested a certain weakness. While his heavy mortars and nebelwerfers were shaking down the store fronts in Bastogne and wounding a few soldiers and civilians, his artillery effort was largely limited to the covering fire given by the tanks and the fire of a relatively few self-propelled guns when his infantry charged forward. This, G-2 attributed to a critical shortage of ammunition.

The cutting of the Neufchâteau road, closing the German circle, appears in the 101st Division records as hardly more than an interesting incident. *[This detail is almost overlooked in all the journals.]* Up till then, the Division's intelligence of the enemy strength and movements was more notable for its blanks than for its specific detailed entries. The G-2 section had, of course, moved cold into an unknown situation and was having to build up its picture of the enemy and friendly forces piece by piece. There had been no pretty "estimates of the situation" to take over and build upon. *[Kinnard and Danahy both stated to Marshall that from their examination of Corps' situation maps upon reaching Bastogne they learned practically nothing of the enemy situation and decided they would have to build from the ground up.]* All that Division could know for certain was what it learned from examining the enemy dead or questioning prisoners. That was enough for Lieutenant Colonel Paul A. Danahy's (Division G-2) main purpose and enough also to satisfy his taste for melodramatic utterance.

Eleven dead men had been found on the ground where the hospital was captured. The corpses had civilian clothes - and German military dogtags. Colonel Danahy went out to make the identifications. A few hours after this find, a message from 10th Armored Division came through Combat Command B to 101st Division Headquarters saying, "You can expect attacks from Sherman tanks, civilians and almost anything now." *[This message was received by Colonel Kinnard and appears in the interview with him. The exact reason for it being sent, however, is not known.]*

Reports came into the G-2 office through the first day of Germans killed while wearing American uniforms and of Sherman tanks pouring fire on our lines. Danahy checked up. He found that invariably, where the enemy used American dress, it was mixed with some of their own clothing, so that they could maintain they were in uniform. *[Danahy was convinced that while using every stratagem possible the enemy was trying to keep within the appearance of acting according to the laws of war for the purpose of protecting their men. He said that the prisoners taken in American uniforms said they had put on this extra clothing to keep from freezing.]* What be had seen gave him fresh inspiration for prophecy.

"Their equipment is augmented by captured U. S. equipment which they do not hesitate to use," he wrote to the commander. "Their morale is excellent but will disintegrate as they come in contact with American airborne troops. It is well known that the Germans dislike fighting. The false courage acquired during their recent successes has so far proved insufficient to prevent their becoming road-bound."

While this message was going out to the regiments of the 101st, the enemy was crossing the Neufchâteau road and cutting the last line to the south, closing the circle around Bastogne. Reconnaissance and combat patrols reported strong enemy infiltrations in the areas west and southwest of the town.

In the morning of December 21, a patrol from Troop D of the 90th Reconnaissance Squadron went down the road to see what the Germans had there. The patrol, under First Lieutenant Arthur

Map 13

B. Arnsdorf, consisted of one tank destroyer and two squads of infantry. They met a group of 101st Division men near Isle-le-Pré (a mile and a half southwest of Bastogne), then moved on some distance farther until they encountered a well emplaced enemy force which made them turn about.

Another armored patrol under Captain Keith J. Anderson went to Clochimont where it observed a large enemy force-riding in American vehicles and dressed in American uniforms.

Later in the morning of December 21 Team Pyle - 14 medium tanks and 200 infantry, mostly from the 9th Armored - moved to the vicinity of Senonchamps to assist the 420th Armored Field Artillery. Lieutenant Colonel Barry D. Browne, in command of the 420th, had received reports that Sibret and Morhet (see map 13) had fallen into enemy hands. He figured that he was out on a limb and that the enemy might come upon him from either

155

flank. So he turned one of his batteries to fire on Sibret and rushed a forward observer out to adjust on the village. At that moment, he saw the motorized column of the 333d Field Artillery Group as it came speeding up the road out of Sibret. Another column came driving hard behind the 333d - men in American clothes and riding American vehicles. They got fairly close to Senonchamps, then stopped, deployed and opened fire with an M8 assault gun.

Even as Colonel Browne realized they were Germans, they started side-slipping off into the Bois de Fragotte which lies just south of Senonchamps. Team Pyle got there in time to help Browne fill those woods with fire; one battery from the 420th Field Artillery Battalion and one from the 755th Field Artillery Battalion (155mms.) also engaged in this action. The infantry and tanks moved west into the woods. Almost immediately, one

Map 14

of the tanks knocked out an enemy 75mm. self-propelled gun. The force then advanced into a large clearing in the center of the forest. While crossing the clearing, one of the tanks was disabled by a shell from a high-velocity gun somewhere in the woods. The tank lost a track. A smoke screen was laid in an attempt to cover its withdrawal, but the tank wouldn't budge and bad to be destroyed.

The force then withdrew to a line farther to the east, but within the forest. Additional support kept coming to it until by night Colonel Browne was commanding 300 infantry and 19 tanks, in addition to running two battalions of artillery. His troops were covering a sector more than 4,000 yards long (see map 14) and running from south of Senonchamps to the Bastogne-Neufchâteau road. All of this had been built up during the day of December 21 as forces were shifted to meet the attack from the new direction. *[Westover's estimate of the position covered.]*

But the heavy increase of fire on the left found Danahy ready to meet the emergency. "The cutting of the roads," he wrote in his periodic report to the commanders that evening, "had had no effect upon our present situation except to make travel hazardous."

14. "NUTS!"

At 1130 ON DECEMBER 22 four Germans, a major, a captain and two enlisted men, came up the road to Bastogne from Remoifosse carrying a large white flag. They were met on the road by Technical Sergeant Oswald Y. Butler and Staff Sergeant Carl E. Dickinson of Company F, 327th Glider infantry, and Private First Class Ernest D. Premetz of the 327th Medical Detachment.

Premetz could speak German. The captain could speak English. He said to Butler, "We are parliamentaires."

The men took the Germans to the house where Lieutenant Leslie E. Smith of Weapons Platoon, Company F, 327th Infantry, had his command post. Leaving the two German enlisted men at the command post, Smith blindfolded the two officers and led them over the hill to the command post of Captain James F. Adams, commanding officer of Company F. Adams called 2d Battalion headquarters in Marvie, Battalion called Regiment in Bastogne, and the 327th Headquarters called the 101st Division, relaying the word that some Germans had come in with surrender terms. The rumor quickly spread around the front that the enemy had had enough and that a party had arrived to arrange a surrender. Quiet held the front. Many of the American defenders crawled out of their cover and spent the noon hour shaving, washing and going to the straddle trenches.

Major Alvin Jones took the terms to General McAuliffe and Lieutenant Colonel Ned D. Moore who was acting Chief of Staff. The paper called for the surrender of the Bastogne garrison and threatened its complete destruction otherwise. It appealed to the "Well known American humanity" to save the people of Bastogne from further suffering. The Americans were to have

Command Post of Company F, 327th Glider Infantry, near Remoifosse. Here the German officer demanding the surrender of Bastogne was blindfolded before being taken to the 327th Glider Infantry Command Post. In the center are Colonel Harper and Major Jones exchanging salutes with the German officers as they were returned to their lines.

two hours in which to consider. The two enemy officers would have to be released by 1400 but another hour would pass before the Germans would resume their attack.

Colonel Harper, commanding the 327th, went with Jones to Division Headquarters. The two German officers were left with Captain Adams. Members of the staff were grouped around General McAuliffe when Harper and Jones arrived. McAuliffe asked someone what the paper contained and was told that it requested a surrender.

He laughed and said, "Aw, nuts!" It really seemed funny to him at the time. He figured he was giving the Germans "one hell of a beating" and that all of his men knew it. The demand was all out of line with the existing situation.

But McAuliffe realized that some kind of reply had to be made and he sat down to think it over. Pencil in hand, he sat there pondering for a few minutes and then he remarked, "Well, I don't know what to tell them." He asked the staff what they thought and Colonel Kinnard, his G-3 replied, "That first remark of yours would be hard to beat."

General McAuliffe didn't understand immediately what Kinnard was referring to. Kinnard reminded him, "You said 'Nuts!'" That drew applause all around. All members of the staff agreed with much enthusiasm and because of their approval McAuliffe decided to send that message back to the Germans.

Then he called Colonel Harper in and asked him how he would reply to the message. Harper thought for a minute but before he could compose anything General McAuliffe gave him the paper on which he had written his one-word reply and asked, "Will you see that it's delivered?" "I will deliver it myself," answered Harper. "It will be a lot of fun." McAuliffe told him not to go into the German lines.

Colonel Harper returned to the command post of Company F. The two Germans were standing in the wood blindfolded and under guard. Harper said, "I have the American commander's reply."

The German captain asked, "Is it written or verbal?"

"It is written," said Harper.

And then be said to the German major, "I will stick it in your hand."

The German captain translated the message. The major then asked, "Is the reply negative or affirmative? If it is the latter I will negotiate further."

All of this time the Germans were acting in an upstage and patronizing manner. Colonel Harper was beginning to lose his temper. He said, "The reply is decidedly not affirmative." Then he added, "If you continue this foolish attack your losses will be tremendous." The major nodded his head.

Harper put the two officers in the jeep and took them back to the main road where the German privates were waiting with the white flag.

He then removed the blindfold and said to them, speaking through the German captain, "If you don't understand what 'Nuts' means, in plain English it is the same as 'Go to hell.' And I will tell you something else - if you continue to attack we will kill every goddam German that tries to break into this city."

The German major and captain saluted very stiffly. The captain said, "We will kill many Americans. This is war." It was then 1350.

"On your way, Bud," said Colonel Harper, "and good luck to you.

The four Germans walked on down the road. Harper returned to the house, regretting that his tongue had slipped and that he had wished them good luck.

The rest of the day was comparatively quiet. The wholesale destruction by artillery that the Germans had promised did not materialize. But, at 1555 there was an attack by some 50 of the enemy against Company F, 327th Glider Infantry, over precisely the same ground where the German mediators had come into our

161

lines. The attack was broken up by small-arms and artillery fire. At 1700 another small attack was again pressed to within 200 yards of Company Fs lines but was beaten back by fire.

The terrain at this spot formed a kind of bowl. The Germans came with their tanks into the bottom of the bowl and fired up against the foxholes along the slope. The men under Sergeant Butler, who had the rifle platoon, and Lieutenant Smith, who had the weapons platoon, held their ground and drove the attackers off with infantry fire alone.

The main event for that day was summed up, though not too neatly, in the G-2 Periodic Report No. 4:

"The Commanding General's answer was, with a sarcastic air of humorous tolerance, emphatically negative. The catastrophic carnage of human lives resulting from the artillery barrage of astronomic proportions which was to be the fate of the defending troops failed to materialize.

"The well known American humanity was considerate of the threatened possible civilian losses by firing artillery concentrations directed at the enemy's impudence."

It was a victory for eloquence at some expense to grammar but in keeping with the other grim humors of the day.

That night, December 22, the Luftwaffe began its bombing attack which was repeated on the next four nights.

15. THE SECOND MARVIE ATTACK

THERE WERE TWO relatively quiet days on the Marvie part of the circular Bastogne front after the snows came - December 21 and 22. Bastogne was searched for enough bedsheets to camouflage the patrols. Early in the afternoon of December 21 the Germans came across the main highway directly south of Bastogne and then began working north toward the battalion lines on the hill.

Colonel Harper shifted the 2d Platoon of Company G, 327th Glider Infantry, from the ground immediately west of Marvie to a place west of the highway. Three of Team O'Hara's tanks were already on the hill where Harper had placed them the day before.

The armor and infantry together were able to turn this thrust back before it became any real threat. *[On the afternoon of December 20 a small task force under 1st Lieutenant Richard C. Gilliland was sent to support 327th along the line covering the main highway. It was called Charlie 16 and included three tanks - two 75mm. and one 76mm. It remained away from the main group for a week, lost the 76mm. tank from a rocket, engaged in 15 skirmishes and destroyed much enemy equipment.]* The 1st Battalion, 327th Glider Infantry, was relieved from attachment to the 501st Airborne Infantry, reverting to direct Division control. It was moved to the southwest of Bastogne in the vicinity of the woods there and ordered to establish a roadblock along the main highway, and from this point to patrol westward to make contact with the 326th Engineer Battalion. They were also instructed to patrol to Villeroux and Chenogne and make contact with "friendly troops"

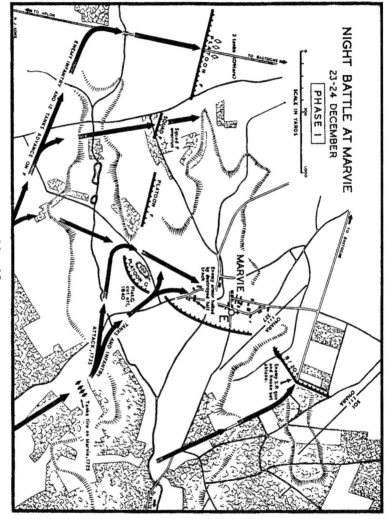

Map 15

but before they could do it the enemy had moved through these positions and driven back the 333d Field Artillery Group. The Engineers then set up as small combat groups and covered the ground between Colonel Hartford F. Salee's 1st Battalion, 327th Glider Infantry, which was over the Neufchâteau road and the platoon from Company G, 327th, which was west of the highway leading south from Bastogne.

In Team O'Hara's part of the sector, too, there was a lull. Some time during the night of December 20 the Germans removed the trees from Team O'Hara's roadblock. At 1100 on the next day a combat patrol went forward to investigate. But on approaching the point where the block had been they found that the enemy now had it covered with crossing bands of machinegun fire. They were able to withdraw without casualty and mortar fire was then put all around the road junction.

In the early hours of December 22 one of Team O'Hara's patrols going forward saw an eleven-man patrol enter their own lines. The night was clear and crisp. The small group from the 54th Armored Infantry first heard the crunching of the snow as the other patrol came toward them. They lay quiet, not firing because they were outnumbered. Too, the strangers were moving as if they were wholly familiar with the ground. They had no visible weapons and they did not carry themselves stealthily. They went boldly over the fences and entered the American lines along the ground that lay between the 327th and the 54th. They walked right by the sentries, moved to within 100 yards of the command post of the 327th Glider Infantry and within 200 yards of the command post of the 54th Armored Infantry.

Four different groups reported the patrol later and all four said they had seen eleven men. Yet the patrol was not challenged anywhere simply because it had moved so confidently. They got in and out without provoking any fire or interest. When Headquarters heard casually how this group had been drifting about, they checked to see whether any nearby unit had put out such a patrol and found that none had done so. Whether the eleven were friend or enemy was never learned. The visitation and its mystery became one of the legends of Bastogne.

At 1725 on December 23, the 2d Battalion, 327th, in Marvie was heavily shelled by enemy tanks concealed in a small plantation of firs within the hollow just above the village of Martaimont. From their position the tanks could shoot directly into Marvie. It was a characteristic enemy action for throughout the siege it was the German practice to use tanks as artillery, perhaps from fear of hitting their own troops if they used field guns from far back. *[This is not the Historian's conclusion but is based on the interview with Colonel Harper and on statements by Major Templeton and Colonel Harper's battalion commanders. Colonel Harper said, "Most of the time when our troops were under shell fire the German gunners were in position to lay directly on the target."]*

At about 1735 the 2d Battalion, 327th, was attacked by tanks and infantry coming from the same general direction (see map 15), though they had debouched from a larger wood lying a little farther away from Marvie. The attack developed very slowly. The German infantry was clad in snow suits and a light snow was falling. They seemed to be waiting until the gloom deepened so they could make the most of their camouflage. The enemy barrage had ignored Team O'Hara's part of the sector but the outposts of the 54th Armored Infantry spotted two enemy machine guns that were firing into Marvie. Flanking fire was placed on them and they were silenced. Heavy automatic fire then searched the position of the 54th. No enemy could be seen and the men of the 54th held their fire except for one heavy machine gun on the left. The enemy spotted that gun. A few minutes later a hand grenade dropped next to the gun killing the gunner and wounding one other man. The rest of the crew quit the position. Next morning a patrol returned to the gun and found the second man still alive but so nearly frozen that he could only nod his head to them. Both he and the dead man had been searched and stripped of their possessions by Germans who had come in fast upon the position after the grenade fire.

Within half an hour the attack was fully developed and soon after 1840, December 23, one platoon of Company G, 327th became surrounded on Hill 500 to the south of Marvie. The enemy had begun a gradual envelopment of the platoon's position by moving into and through houses and yards that were around the base of the hill on all sides. A few members of the platoon were able to withdraw along the flanks of the hill as the encirclement began. The others stayed in their positions and the time quickly came when they could not get out. *[Colonel Harper later had this to say of what happened to Morrison, "I'll never again put infantry on a forward slope unless I have tank destroyers or tanks where I can protect them. I lost two platoons separately in defense of the perimeter by making this mistake. In each case they were overrun when there were no tank destroyers to defend them."]*

Four tanks, which had accompanied the German infantry advance to Hill 500, turned their fire against Marvie, adding to the bombardment that was still coming in from the armored guns in the big wood.

Colonel Harper had worried about this part of the perimeter. Earlier in the day he had asked Colonel O'Hara to put a tank on the hill. O'Hara agreed to station a 57mm. gun on the lower slope of the hill where a 37mm. gun had previously defended it. The half-track carrying the 57mm. gun was just going into position when the German tanks and infantry closed in on Hill 500. The first few German rounds that came his way were enough for the driver; he turned the half-track around and sped north toward Marvie. The troops in the village saw the half-track coming toward them from out of the body of the German attack. They thought it was a German vehicle and they fired at it with everything they had, demolishing the vehicle and killing the crew. Two German tanks that had followed along the same road crossed the stream south of Marvie and got into the village as far as the church. They saw then that the destroyed half-track blocked the road and that they could not advance any farther. So they turned around and withdrew. *[This incident was related during the interview with Colonel Harper and supported by the battalion commander. It was not brought to light, however, during Westover's conversations with Colonel O'Hara's force.]*

Having begun the attack in stealth, the German infantry now came on toward the houses in a frenzy, yelling and firing as they advanced and shooting many flares. To the men in Colonel O'Hara's position it looked as if the tracers were flying in all directions. Bullet fire began to envelop them from the southern edge of the village. A self-propelled gun came charging toward them up the Wiltz road. As it rounded the bend and came abreast the farmhouse there, one of our medium tanks fired and the gun went up in flames. The fire lighted the entire area. The enemy turned their artillery loose on the farmhouse. A loft filled with hay soon blazed like a torch. Because of the intense illumination from these fires, the tanks and infantry of Team O'Hara's line withdrew 100 yards to the west.

Counting an Engineer platoon on the right of Colonel Harper's 327th Glider Infantry, there were 98 men defending Hill 500. Already, a few had been killed or wounded. At the same time that a part of the German force pressed against Marvie from the south, twelve German tanks supported by infantry advanced north along the main road toward the position occupied by Company F, 327th. This body had debouched from the same woods from which the German tanks were firing. Instead of continuing along the Bastogne road, part of the German armor moved rightward toward Hill 500. The infantry were clad in white and were almost imperceptible.

On the slopes of Hill 500 Lieutenant Stanley Morrison and his men of Company G, 327th Glider Infantry, had dug in around the base of the houses. Colonel Harper in his command post got word that the enemy was attacking. He called Lieutenant Morrison and asked, 'What is your situation?"

"Now they are all around me," Morrison replied. "I see tanks just outside my window. We are continuing to fight them back but it looks like they have us." To Colonel Harper's listening ear he seemed perfectly calm and he spoke in a level tone.

Harper called him back in about three minutes. Morrison replied but he said only these words, "We're still holding on." Then the line went dead.

Lieutenant Colonel Thomas J. Rouzie, the executive officer of the 327th Glider Infantry, said to Harper, "I guess that's the end of Morrison."

The men of Hill 500 were never heard from again in the battle. They had been overwhelmed by troops of the 901st Panzergrenadier Regiment of the Panzer Lehr Division. The end came for Lieutenant Morrison's detachment some time after 1900, December 23. *[Morrison's body was not found and it was hoped that he was taken prisoner. Both Harper and Rouzie recalled the words of the conversations.]*

There had been no tanks or tank destroyers in support of Morrison. Force O'Hara had not fired either in defense of the hill positions or against the German front moving into Marvie from the south. Colonel Harper couldn't understand it. He called Colonel O'Hara who said, "They are attacking me also and are trying to come around my north flank."

This flank had a patch of woods lying just north of the bend of the road but not within the American position and the enemy was striking from out of those woods. Now the snow suits no longer helped them for they reflected the light of the blazing house. From 100 yards away O'Hara's men fired. Some of the figures pitched forward in the snow and others sought its concealment.

One of Colonel O'Hara's men had failed to withdraw in time.

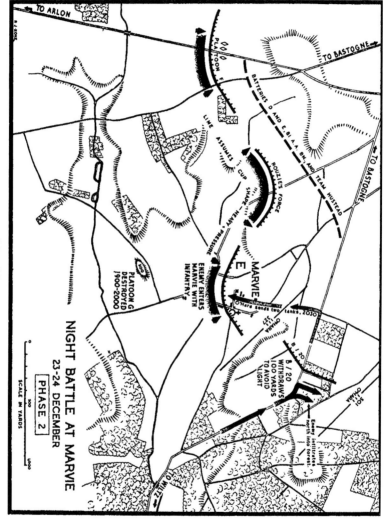

Map 16

NIGHT BATTLE AT MARVIE
23-24 DECEMBER
PHASE 2

SCALE IN YARDS
0   500   1000

He played dead when the Germans came to his foxhole. They said, "Hello, Hello," then kicked him, sat on him, took his BAR and rifled his pockets. But he kept absolutely still. Some time later be heard them bring up two guns on the left, a large one and a small one. They fired the small gun indiscriminately, apparently with the expectation of getting return fire which would provide a target for the large gun. Yet during the night the large gun never did fire. The man in the foxhole also heard the German ambulances make numerous trips into the area for the purpose of taking out their dead and wounded.

Major Galbreaith (executive officer of the 2d Battalion, 327th), reported to Colonel Harper at 2000, December 23, that the German infantry were in the south end of Marvie and were working through the houses. (see Map 16) The tanks which had been on Hill 500 and had shelled Marvie from there were now moving toward the houses. Galbreaith asked Harper, "Can't I get tanks?" Harper replied, "I'll try." But the line to Team O'Hara had gone out. Colonel Harper tried the radio but could only hear Team O'Hara headquarters faintly.

Major Galbreaith called Colonel Harper again, and said, "They are all around us now and I must have tanks."

"You call O'Hara on your radio," replied Harper, "and say 'It is the commanding general's order that two Sherman tanks move into Marvie at once and take up a defensive position.'"

Colonel Harper had no authority for his action but be figured this wasn't the time to stand on ceremony. A few minutes later the two Sherman tanks moved into Marvie on Colonel O'Hara's orders. The infantry of both sides were already locked in a fight for possession of the houses but the destroyed half-track kept the enemy armor from entering the south of the village.

Colonel Harper's force was now totally stripped of reserve. His line was buckled in and from Hill 500 the Germans were in good position to exploit the break in his center, roll back the flanks of his position, and through this breach enter the heart of

Bastogne. But once again in renewing their direct assault on the city the Germans had made the same error of engaging heavily only along one part of the front. The front at Foy bad cooled off and Colonel Ewell's forces along the Longvilly road could even doze a little. *[This general estimate of situation is supported by all the records and interviews.]*

At 2145 a platoon of paratroopers from Company A of the 501st Parachute Infantry under Captain Stanfield A. Stach was sent to reinforce Company F of the 327th Glider Infantry. That company was already in a pretty bad way. One of its squads had been in the small patch of woods just to the southwest of Hill 500 and part of a platoon had been on higher ground to the squad's right rear. These positions had been overrun by the German armored advance from out of the woods around Martaimont.

A few of the men got away. Others had been killed or taken prisoner defending their ground. The bulk of the company, in position along the crest of the hill commanding the main highway into Bastogne from the south, had held like a rock. The German assault had come on with its right closing around Marvie, its center enveloping Hill 500 and its left lunging forward along the main highway. The armor that supported the advance of the German left could be stopped only by bazooka fire from Lieutenant Smith's platoon, for this was no place for tank destroyers. Anything that came over the skyline of the hill moving southward from Bastogne was immediately put under fire by German tanks or self-propelled guns firing from defilade. No tank destroyers could be risked at the position. Three of Colonel O'Hara's tanks, known as Force Charley 16, were in support of our infantry line, but the night attack closed in in such manner that the fate of the line depended on the infantry weapons. There was a respite after Smith's fire beat back the first attack but the enemy tanks withdrew only a short distance.

The ruptured line north of Hill 500 was quickly patched and

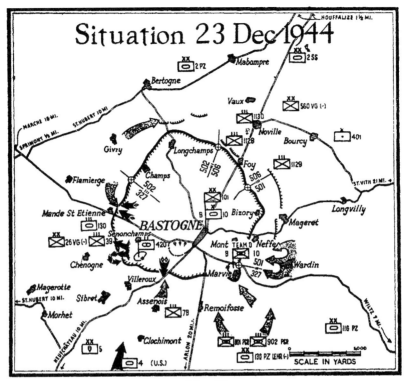

Map 17

strengthened before the enemy could exploit his opening success. One platoon of Company F, which had been astride the Bastogne road, was put in position to east of it (see Map 17). The 327th Glider Infantry was also given Batteries D and E of the 81st Antiaircraft Battalion and Major Hustead's part of Team Cherry. Twelve guns were put in an arc along the high ground in the road triangle just above Marvie.

Colonel Rouzie picked up twenty-four men of Company F and with the forty men under Captain Stach proceeded through Lieutenant Smith's position and took up a defense line corresponding with the distribution of the 81st's antiaircraft guns. These moves - made between 2400 and 0100 (December 24) - temporarily closed the breach. Colonel Rouzie took personal charge of the defense of the threatened area. Upon reaching the ground he had decided he was in no position to attack. He felt that he would simply waste his strength if he tried to drive the Germans away from Hill 500. The best course open was to establish a defensive line on the "inner part of the cup."41 Captain Adams reorganized the position of Company F so that the line bent back northeastward to join with the position covering the 81st's guns. *[Adams's command post was on the west side of the Bastogne road across from Smith's.]*

Twice again that night the German armor lashed at the left flank and always the fire fell heaviest, not on Colonel Rouzie's scratch force, but on the position held by the platoons of Lieutenant Smith and Technical Sergeant Butler. The regimental officers of the 327th Glider Infantry said later that Sergeant Butler's courage and energy were the mainstay of the defense. In one of the assaults a pair of German tanks got to within fifty yards of the foxholes held by Lieutenant Smith's men before they were turned back by bazooka fire. By then Smith's command post was blazing, for the tanks had fired fifteen rounds into the house as they came on. Smith and his assistants had set up in the basement and they stayed there while the upper structure burned.

Rouzie's force patrolled southward to the small woods from where part of Company F had been driven and found that it was now held by an enemy outpost. A few Company F stragglers were trying to work their way out of the woods. The patrol mistook them for Germans and fired on them. They hit the ground. One member of the patrol, suspecting that they were Americans, crawled forward, identified them and brought them out. The enemy had captured a number of American mortars around Marvie and through the rest of the night American mortar shells dropped on the ground which Smith and Butler were defending. In the early morning the Germans asked and received permission to remove their dead and wounded from in front of Smith's platoon. It was only when the Germans came forward to collect their dead that the pressure slackened and the mortar fire ceased.

Elsewhere along the sector the issue of the fight was still in balance. Two tanks which had ripped through Harper's forward line had gone right into Bastogne and shot up the houses around his command post, without doing any vital damage. In Marvie the arrival of the two Sherman tanks had stabilized the fighting.

Near midnight, December 23, as the Shermans rolled south into the village, they could hear German armor coming north. They could not see the force nor tell its numbers but the muzzle flashes told them they were engaged at very short range. Again the dead half-track helped save the situation. The leading German tank got up to this accidental roadblock and then tried to turn around, but was knocked out by the two Shermans before it could do so. This loss checked the rest of the enemy armor.

Colonel Harper's infantry in Marvie bad dug themselves in very deep right next to the foundations of the houses and they stayed in their holes without flinching. They now had all the best of it because the village was blazing from many fires set by the artillery. Their foxholes were in heavy shadow while the snow-suited German infantry were highlighted as they came across the open spaces. The general assault was quickly checked by bullet fire but enemy parties got a lodgment in the houses at the lower end of the village and pushed slowly northward.

Along Team O'Hara's front things had quieted well before midnight. The enemy advance into the fire-lighted area was checked and then driven back by machine-gun and rifle fire. Later, after the scene bad again darkened, an enemy tank was heard advancing along the road. The artillery forward observer fired the 75mm. gun from his tank and a 105mm. assault gun fired in the direction of the rumble. Second Lieutenant Sherwood D. Wishart, tank platoon leader, reported that night that he was certain his shells had bounced off and the tank bad backed away. But he had scored a bull's-eye in the darkness and in the morning the tank - a Mark IV - was found sitting to the left of the road with a 75mm. hole clear through it. Not a single body was found on the ground which had been held by the enemy infantry, though the snow bore many other marks of death and confusion. The German medical units had done their tasks well. *[Colonel O'Hara made a thorough search in the interests of identification.]*

Soon after dawn of December 24 Colonel Harper went down to look at his lines. He sent a patrol to the hill where Lieutenant Morrison had been and found it was still in enemy bands. His own men still held most of Marvie though the Germans were in some houses in the south of the village. Five men had been killed and seven wounded in the fighting there and one and one-half platoons had been wiped out on the hill. There were no further developments in the situation during the morning.

At 0900 a patrol from Colonel O'Hara's force went to the old roadblock position and found that the enemy bad withdrawn except for two Germans who were sitting fully exposed on a nearby pile of beets. They shot the two beet sitters and this drew machine-gun fire on themselves. So they pulled back.

At 1340 six P-47s bombed Marvie, dropping six 500-pound bombs among the American positions. Then they came in over the housetops and strafed the streets with caliber .50 fire. Colonel Harper was walking through the streets when the first bomb fell. Even as he jumped for a foxhole he saw that there were two cerise-colored panels clearly showing where the front of the position was. He thought he saw one of the bombs bit among a patrol that was working through the south of the village toward Hill 500 and he sent two runners after the patrol to see if any damage had been done. Then he walked in the same direction. A German wearing a dirty snow suit dodged out of one house and into another so that he could get into a position from which he could fire on the patrol. Harper fired his M1 at the house in order to warn the patrol. The patrol, which seemed OK from the bombing, went to work on the house too, but on receiving rifle fire from the south of the village, they came on back.

During their brief reconnaissance they bad seen a German tank completely camouflaged as a haystack except that the Germans had made the error of leaving the gun muzzle sticking out of the hay. Colonel Harper went to the one Sherman tank remaining in the village and gave the gunner the target - just beyond the last houses. He continued on to the tanks of Team O'Hara along the Wiltz road and told them to start pounding the tank and the houses in the lower part of Marvie which concealed the German infantry. With their first fire the Shermans got direct hits on the tank and blew the hay away. They kept on blasting it and the crews thought they knocked it out. Major Galbreaith (2d Battalion Exec, 327th) said, however, that he saw the tank get away under its own power.

At 1645 the P-47 planes returned again and attacked Marvie with bombs and bullets.59 At 1945 Bastogne was bombed and strafed by several enemy planes.

At 1800, December 24, Colonel Harper was told that he was in command of the perimeter all the way from Marvie to northwest of Hemroulle.

Colonel Harper said to General Higgins, "Look at it! This is half of the Division perimeter."

General Higgins replied, "It's all yours. Do what you can with it. There isn't any other solution."

Higgins reasoned that it was a fairly safe gamble. He had studied the map carefully and had gleaned all that he could from firsthand study of the country just outside the Bastogne perimeter. The landscape to the south was heavily wooded and therefore not suitable for armor. He considered that the only place where the enemy was likely to strike Harper's sector in force was at the Wiltz road. But the opening there was a pretty narrow corridor and he felt that Harper had enough strength across the Wiltz road to deal with any fresh threat at that point. What concerned General Higgins most was the position in the northwest sector, a gently rolling hill country, with no natural obstacles and very little tree growth. Thus far it had been the quietest portion of the perimeter but that fact did not lessen Higgins' apprehension; he felt sure that if a real tank stroke was coming, this would be the point of danger. He remarked to General McAuliffe that they could expect to be entertained out there on Christmas Day.

"The Germans are a sentimental people," he said, "and they are probably thinking about giving a present to Hitler."

16. LOW EBB OF SUPPLY

DESPITE the deceptively inactive appearance of the front, the defenders of Bastogne had actually reached the lowest ebb of their fortune by the night of December 22. The crisis was a matter of supply. *[General McAuliffe says that December 23 was the day of crisis. In this he appears to be mistaken. The artillery commanders all said that it was on the afternoon of the 22d that they were most worried about their supply. This checks with the fact that resupply began to arrive fairly early the next morning.]*

General McAuliffe's confidence thus far had been well founded. In manpower, he had been able to maintain a very favorable balance between his reserves and his deployments. His infantry losses had been light. The circle of defenses had been scarcely dented. The German forces, which as a whole had been rapidly moving in the Bulge offensive elsewhere, had so signally failed to put on a coordinated attack against his all-around front that he had been able to beat down each of their separate thrusts by massing the fire of his artillery.

The gun pits of all the defending 105mm. batteries were complete circles. At different times during the siege nearly all guns fired around the whole 6,400 mils of the compass. Most of the artillery fired in support of each infantry battalion against every major attack the Germans made. *[From Colonel Marshall's interviews with Lieutenant Colonel John T. Cooper, Jr., and Colonel Nelson, and from General McAuliffe's statement on the employment of his artillery.]*

More than that, however, the artillery could not do. All day long the infantry commanders witnessed the enemy build-up opposite their sectors. Tanks and half-tracks loaded with German infantry moved freely and contemptuously along the lateral roads, making no effort at concealment although they were within easy range of the howitzers. It made the defenders frantic.

For by noon of December 22 the 463d Field Artillery Battalion, which was supporting the 327th Glider Infantry, had only 200 rounds of ammunition left and the other battalions were in a similar plight. During the first three days there bad been shells enough. Now, in the face of the enemy build-up, the pinch was really hurting and General McAuliffe was about at the point where he would have to ration his guns to ten rounds per day.

There was a delightfully ironic touch even to that restriction, for the supply had dropped very low indeed. Checking the battalions on that day, Colonel Sherburne, the artillery commander, found that with the exception of one battalion which had several hundred rounds of short-range 105mm. ammunition which it alone was equipped to fire, the batteries were down to less than ten rounds total per gun. Still, he kept his own counsel, and when men and officers asked him how the general supply of artillery ammunition was faring, he lied cheerfully and skillfully. At times members of the staff became confused between the true figures and the figures which Sherburne was quoting publicly for the sake of morale. The shell shortage continued to be General McAuliffe's worst, in fact, his only real worry. He told his batteries not to fire "until you see the whites of their eyes."

The infantry commanders and the few remaining artillery observers screamed their heads off about it. One commander phoned General McAuliffe, "We are about to be attacked by two regiments. We can see them out there. Please let us fire at least two rounds per gun."

Colonel Kinnard listened to this plea and later recalled General McAuliffe's reply, "If you see 400 Germans in a 100-yard area, and they have their heads up, you can fire artillery at them - but not more than two rounds.

At the same time, the Bastogne defenders were running low on small-arms ammunition. *[General McAuliffe recollected this as happening on December 23. Colonel Kinnard said it happened on December 22. The 22d appears to be correct inasmuch as resupply became assured on the morning of December 23. There is no doubt, however, about the validity of this quotation. Kinnard and Danahy both heard it, and when his memory was refreshed General McAuliffe recalled that he had said it.]*

So with somewhat mixed feelings the word was received among the regiments at 1530 on that evening that a column from the 4th Armored Division was coming up from the southwest to support the 101st Airborne Division and would be able to give the 101st relief in time.

It was still a neat question whether that relief would come before the ammunition ran out.

In the smaller units which were attachments to the 101st perhaps the strain was even greater. *[Westover was impressed by this difference in how the little units looked at the operation as compared with the 101st Division Headquarters viewpoint. The observation was made on the basis of Westover's findings as contrasted with Marshall's.]* Confidence can come of numbers around the headquarters of a large organization. Talking with his staff, General McAuliffe gained the impression that none doubted the outcome. But out on the fire line, friends shook bands as the darkness came, figuring that all might be overwhelmed before morning. They could take no measure of the reserve strength of the position. What they saw was how few rounds per gun they had left and how large were the numbers of the enemy. The paratroopers were somewhat accustomed to being surrounded by enemy, but it was a new experience for the units who stood with them, unwavering.

The first message from the 4th Armored said, "Hugh is coming." When General McAuliffe had visited General Middleton (commander of VIII Corps) in Neufchâteau on the night of December 20, he had been told that General Patton was attacking east of Bastogne. The two commanders then set up a simple code, each town along the route getting a letter. Bastogne was "K." Others were designated A, B, C. Now the word was that "Hugh *[Major General Hugh J. Gaffey, commanding the 4th Armored Division]* is on his way."

On the heels of that assurance came another message equally bright. VIII Corps radioed that pathfinders, would arrive in Bastogne at 1600 and that resupply by air would start coming in at 2000. Colonel Kohls, G-4, 101st Division, had waited all day long for that appointment, for on the day before VIII Corps had told him to prepare for "resupply tomorrow if weather permits."

Directly west of the houses of Bastogne are large, clear fields on a gentle hillside, close to where the 101st Division had made its command post. This was the designated spot.

Under average operating conditions resupply bundles are recovered by Quartermaster and Ordnance companies and their items of matériel are then segregated in Class I, III and V dumps under Division control. At Bastogne, Colonel Kohls had no Division supply forces available either to pick up the resupply or manage the distribution. The regiments were therefore told to send at least five quarter-ton trucks to the field to handle the supplies directly and haul them to unit dumps. The units were told to report what supplies they had each recovered and then to distribute them according to orders which would be given by the G-4 Section.

At 0730 on December 22, the task of recovering the aerial resupply was given to Major William H. Butler, S-4 of the 501st Parachute Infantry, and Captain Matheson, S-4 of the 506th.

They went to the drop zone, got the crews and vehicles alerted, put out the panels to guide the plane and then waited.

Nothing happened during the day. In the late afternoon came the message from VIII Corps. At 1605 Corps said that the pathfinders would be dropped at 1723 and that the flight would be two planes with ten men each. Captain John M. Huffman, Assistant to G-4, went at once to the drop zone to notify Major Butler. However, at 1641 the operation was cancelled because of ice conditions.

Then the Division rear base radioed at 1700 that sixty C-47s would drop supplies on the first flyable day. However, VIII Corps had not yet given up. At 2115, it radioed that an attempt de will be made to drop a portion of the supplies."

Colonel Kohls again alerted Butler who went to the drop zone and put out the fluorescent panels. Nothing happened. Out of great expectation came only great disappointment.

17. SUPPLIES ARRIVE

FROM DAYLIGHT ON December 23 all guards stood alerted for the first appearance of the C-47s. At 0935 a military policeman on duty at the entrance to the 101st Division command post carried the word to Colonel Kohls that several large planes were circling the area.

A few minutes later, the pathfinders jumped in the area where the 2d Battalion of Colonel Harper's 327th Glider Infantry was deployed. They were quickly rounded up by his men. One minute later, First Lieutenant Gordon O. Rothwell, commanding the pathfinder team, was on the telephone explaining to Colonel Kohls that the supply planes would arrive in about 90 minutes. Kohls told him how to get to the drop zone and where to put the radar set. Again the regimental supply men were alerted. Again Major Butler displayed the panels. At 1150 on the 23d, men all along the front saw the planes coming in; it was the most

Medicine, food and ammunition being dropped from C-47s to the defenders of Bastogne.

Members of the 101st Airborne Division bring in a supply bundle.
Recovery ran as high as 95% and the bundles were utilized immediately.

heartening spectacle of the entire siege.

Men and vehicles were all set for it. The pathfinder radar had given Captain Huffman and Lieutenant Colonel John T. Cooper, Jr. (Commanding Officer, 463d Parachute Field Artillery Battalion) a half-hour advance warning that the planes were coming in and the supply parties reached the field ten minutes before the flight, in time for Huffman to assign zones of retrieving to each unit so that there would be a uniformly quick pick-up. There was very little enemy fire on any part of the field.

Sixteen planes arrived in the first flight, but these were just the beginning. By 1606 of that day, 241 planes had dropped 1446 bundles weighing 144 tons by parachute into the milesquare drop zone. The drop pattern was excellent and there was about a 95 per cent recovery of the dropped material.

Working against the approaching darkness, the supply crews threw whole bundles, parachute and all, into the jeeps and shuttled between the drop zone and their dumps as fast as they could tear over the ground. All supplies were in the unit dumps by 1700, and even before that time ammunition had been rushed directly to the front lines and the battery positions. The artillery was firing part of the resupply ammunition at the enemy before the drop zone had been cleared.

By the time darkness came on, Colonel Kohls had at hand reports from all the unit supply officers telling what quantities of matériel had reached their unit dumps. It took only a brief checking on his part to see that his supply problem was far from being solved. The contents of the bundles were not in balance with the real needs of the troops. They still desperately lacked certain items and they had received others which they did not need or want. A great amount of caliber .50 ammunition had been sent up but this was not much in demand. The new supply of caliber .30 for the M1, and of 76mm. APC and 75mm. ammunition was insufficient. The Division needed litters and penicillin badly and though it had collected all of the available bed clothing from the Belgian community, many of its men were still miserably cold at night and were asking for blankets.

Colonel Kohls talked to VIII Corps again at 0830 the next morning (December 24) and said he wanted these things. He asked for additional quantities of ammunition for the 75mm. pack howitzer and also of 105mm. M3 shell. He asked VIII Corps to investigate the possibility of using gliders in the further resupply. All the early resupply missions had been done by parachute. As they came in the Germans put up a terrific amount of flak. The troops saw a number of C-47s shot down, but these losses had not made other planes take evasive action. Colonel Harper said of the pilots who flew these missions:

"Their courage was tremendous, and I believe that their example did a great deal to encourage my infantry."

While Kohls was talking, the first resupply planes of the day appeared over the drop zone and more bundles continued to rain down on the field until 1530. About 100 tons of matériel were parachuted out of 160 planes during that second day of resupply. Even so, the Division's stocking was not by any means full as Christmas Eve drew on. The shortages weighed more on Colonel Kohls than what had been accomplished. Onlv 445 gallons of gasoline were on hand. The 26,406 K rations that had been received were only enough to supply the defenders of Bastogne for a little more than a single day. The troops were instructed, for a second time, to forage for any food supplies in their areas and to report them to G-4 so that they could be distributed where they were needed most.

This bad been done from the beginning and a large part of the subsistence of the defense had come from the ruined stores of Bastogne or from the stocks of the farming community. From an abandoned Corps bakery had come flour, lard, salt and a small quantity of coffee. Colonel Kohls got these things out to the troops and during the first days of the siege the favorite menu item along the firing line was flapjacks. The coffee, however, was saved for the hospital. The farmers had fairly good supplies

This 155mm M1A1 howitzer has just received ammunition from the glider in the background. This incident occurred during the siege of Bastogne.

of potatoes, poultry and cattle. These were taken over on requisition, to be paid for later by the United States. In an abandoned Corps warehouse were found another 450 pounds of coffee, 600 pounds of sugar and a large amount of Ovaltine. These things were all hoarded for the wounded. Prowling about Bastogne, the Civil Affairs Officer, Captain Robert S. Smith, found a large store of margarine, jam and flour in a civilian warehouse. This assured flapjacks for several more days. What was equally important, he found 2,000 burlap bags among the groceries and the bags were rushed out to the infantrymen in the foxholes to wrap around their feet where they lacked arctic overshoes.

By Christmas Eve these supplementary stores were pretty well exhausted. Christmas was a K-ration day - for the men who had K rations.

18. THE SITUATION IMPROVES

WITHOUT FULLY REALIZING IT, the defenders of Bastogne passed their crisis on December 23. They could not measure the change, nor did they know how many elements were acting in their favor. But quite suddenly everything began to come their way. This was not a matter alone of successful local tactics against the enemy. Nor was it only that the measures taken by the VIII Corps and the larger forces concerned with the relief of the defenders were at last beginning to bear fruit, as evidenced by the arrival of the resupply missions. For one thing, such a vital matter as the weather continued to favor the defense.

In the beginning there had been fog and acute dampness which appeared at first blush to doubly jeopardize the situation of a force that was having to feel its way to the enemy and was suffering from shortages of clothing and blankets. Yet all that happened in the opening encounters during the first two days Bastogne's fate was in the balance proved that the atmosphere served almost as a protecting screen for the defenders and wrought confusion among the oncoming forces.1 Had there not been fog of course there could have been air support. But it is a question whether that support could have been greatly effective during a period when it would have been difficult to distinguish between the retreating remnants of the broken American divisions and the advancing German columns. Again, an early intervention by the air power might have forestalled those concentrations of German armor and other vehicles which were to provide such inviting targets when the opening at last came.

On December 19 Captain James E. Parker, of the Ninth Air Force, reported into Bastogne as air controller for the defense.

Map 17

His equipment consisted of a pocket full of radio crystals; what he needed was a high frequency radio that would give him contact with American planes. He searched the whole 101st Division without success, then found that the attached 10th Armored Division units had two radios of the type needed - one in a tank and the other in a jeep. The tank could not be spared but the jeep and a technician from Ninth Air Force, Sergeant Frank B. Hotard, were given to Captain Parker. By December 21 his radio equipment was complete and he was ready to work with supporting planes. But the fog still enveloped Bastogne to keep the planes away. Parker had to wait two more days.

While the fog held, the first snow flurries came and the weather grew increasingly cold. On the night of December 21 came the first heavy snowfall, adding to the hardships of the front-line troops and the hazards of patrolling. The overcast was still thick and the ground fog irregular. On the morning of December 23, for the first time since the Bastogne defenders were committed to action, a day dawned fair and clear though with freezing temperatures. It looked like the hour of opportunity.

By then the defenses of Bastogne had become so closely knit, and there was such complete harmony and mutual confidence among the oddly assorted groups of the defense, that it seemed certain that all of the changes in the natural conditions of the battlefield would work only to the disadvantage of the enemy. The defensive lines were set. The crisp clear air insured that if the Germans came on, their snow-suit camouflage would not be overly helpful; at least their features and their weapons could be seen. *[This conclusion is drawn from numerous conversations the historians had with front line troops.]* The roads from Bastogne to all parts of the perimeter were like the spokes of a wheel. They were generally good roads. But particularly around the northern half of the defense they entered the perimeter over ground where a stout roadblock might well hold up an armored regiment for hours. The German armor and its support had largely held to the roads during the period of build-up; and they were still out there, daring the lightning. Wire communications from Bastogne command post to all parts of the perimeter were working as strongly on behalf of the defense as was the axial highway system. Only a few times had the wire gone out. The 101st's practice of emphasizing a net of lateral wires, which set up several ways of reaching the outfits on the perimeter, had saved a number of situations that might otherwise have been blacked out. And foresightedly, the Signal Company had brought in plenty of extra wire.

Now that there was the sure prospect of air resupply, the artillery situation was looking up. It had suffered thus far only from its fears that the ammunition wouldn't last. By the 22d, General McAuliffe's supply had dropped down to twenty-odd rounds per gun and Colonel Roberts' about as low, and some guns were down to ten rounds. But both commanders were certain that as long as the artillery ammunition lasted, Bastogne would hold.

The opening engagements had reaffirmed the power of an ample artillery properly directed, and by committing their forces piecemeal the Germans had played right into the hands of the defense which had staked its life on the massed fire of its guns. The guns of Combat Command B, 10th Armored Division, were capable of getting 11,000 yards out of their 105mm. ammunition while the same ammunition in the short 105 tubes of the Airborne Artillery units could only reach about 4,500 yards. The Armored Artillery was therefore the real power of the defense together with the twenty 155mm. howitzers of the Artillery battalions that had been caught in the town(the 755th and part of the 333d Field Artillery Group).

During the first stage, the great natural strength of the position and the vast superiority of the American artillery had worked together for the salvation of Bastogne. The German artillery had been little more than a cipher, save for the fire from the tanks and self-propelled guns. At times it seemed to consist of single guns and their shoots were never very long. The town itself had not yet been given any steady shelling by the enemy guns and the command posts were able to maintain their liaison with little difficulty.

This lack of power in the German artillery and the inability of the German foot and armor to coordinate their assaults against different parts of the perimeter-probably because their communication system had broken under the pressures of the advance-minimized the moral strain which would normally afflict a body of troops that found itself surrounded. The command and staff of the defense were not feeling what they had expected to feel from the lessons they had learned at Leavenworth and Benning. They knew they were cut off. The

G-2 reports and the incessant patrol activities against all portions of the defensive circle told them so. But they did not feel cut off. They remained mobile and mentally able to promote all of the tactical advantages of their interior position. The thought that there were Germans all around them brought no particular extra worry. They were confident that help from the outside was just around the corner.

However, the most decisive gains of the period had been in the work of the fighting men themselves and in their feeling about one another. In the beginning the different elements of the defense were almost out of communication one with the other. Things had happened so fast that they had been compelled to engage the enemy before giving a thought to their own liaison. But in the course of battle the infantry, the armored force and the tank destroyer crews had taken full measure of each other and found the measure sufficient. The birth of mutual confidence and respect had produced not only tactical cohesion but comradeship in such a degree that before the siege was over these units were to ask their higher commanders whether it wouldn't be possible for them to be joined permanently in one large force. They had come to believe that together they had become irresistible.

After their first tilt in which each had spoken bluntly and made his point, General McAuliffe and Colonel Roberts tabled their feelings and worked together to perfect the team play of their respective forces. As McAuliffe's advisor on armor, Roberts found himself among "the best and keenest staff" he had ever seen. Not only did they radiate extreme confidence but they proved to be "great bird dogs" in detecting early enemy build-ups. As soon as the first signs of an enemy attack became apparent, Colonel Roberts would alert his Division reserve and get it moving toward the likely area of irruption. He would then concern himself with building another Division reserve. He never bothered General McAuliffe with these details. If it chanced that Colonel Cherry, the Division reserve commander, got cut up, or if the 101st Division troops moved over during an action and drew parts of Team Cherry into the front line, there was always Team O'Hara with 14 tanks which he could get out of line quickly in case of necessity.

Colonel Roberts' force had more than paid for itself during the first two days. He had taken his greatest losses in tanks and men in the opening engagement, but that sacrifice had staved off the Germans and gained the exact amount of time needed for the 101st to establish itself solidly. After the first two days Colonel Roberts' two chopped-up teams were consolidated as one and this part of the force became his Division reserve. The number of tanks available for it varied from day to day between six and ten.

Lieutenant Colonel Templeton, the Tank Destroyer commander (705th Battalion), took hold in the same strong way, an even having his men fight as infantrymen when they could not be employed otherwise. On the other hand he was never loath to make his point strongly any time he thought the higher commanders were planning to make an unwise employment of his forces.3Colonel Templeton's command post was only a hundred yards from the command post of the 101st Division, so coordination was simple. In turn he received from the battalion commanders of the 101st the kind of support that rewarded all of his effort. During relief periods the infantry platoons covering his tank destroyers made the security of Templeton's guns their first concern.

Colonel Roberts, too, was learning from Templeton as they went along. He had reached the conclusion that, properly employed in a defense like Bastogne, some tanks must be up with the infantry and some in reserve in the "socker" role. But what bothered him was the discovery that while his tankers were actually having to work as tank destroyers about 98 per cent of the time, the tank destroyer men seemed so much better trained to get away with it. This was strongly reflected in the ratio of losses in the two forces when compared with the damage done to the enemy armor.

At 1000 on December 23 Captain Parker at his radio heard that supporting planes were on their way. Within a few minutes he was telling them where to strike. The strongest enemy buildups at this time were west and northwest of the town, threatening the sectors held by the 502d Parachute Infantry and the 327th Glider Infantry regiments. The infantry front lines had been hearing and seeing the arrival of these concentrations during the past two days. But because of the shortage of artillery ammunition, there had been no real check against them. The planes dropped low and came in fast against the enemy columns, gaining complete surprise. The German vehicles were on the road facing toward Bastogne when the first bombs fell among them. Such was the execution that one of the pilots later said to General McAuliffe, "This was better hunting than the Falaise pocket and that was the best I ever expected to see." *[As for the extent of the enemy build-up in the northwest, Colonel Chappuis says in the 502d Parachute Infantry interview that the most trying thing in those days on his troops was that they had to look out every day and see enemy trucks and men swarming up and down the roads all around them. He said, "We could have murdered those Germans. The road intersections in front of us looked like 42d and Broadway after a football game. Most of the traffic seemed to be moving to the west. They were in easy reach and were quite contemptuous about it. But we could do nothing about it because we did not have the artillery ammunition."]*

On that first day the Germans did not use their antiaircraft guns against any of the dive bombers. If this reticence was due to a desire to cover up the positions of the guns, it was a view quickly changed because of the damage the Ninth Air Force planes had done during the first day. For thereafter the German flak was intense over the front at all times and the air units had no further hours of unopposed operation.

They made the most of their opening opportunity. The snow was a great aid. Clearly visible tracks pointed to forest positions which were promptly bombed. The fir forests burst into flames from the fire bombs and before the day was out the smoke from these blazing plantations and from the brewed-up enemy columns made a complete circle around the besieged forces until it seemed almost as if the fog was closing in again. The air people hit every nearby town at least once with explosive and fire bombs. Noville was hit ten times.

The entire air operation was carefully systematized and then supervised in detail. As planes were assigned to the 101st Division by VIII Corps, they checked in with Captain Parker by radio. He put them on a clear landmark such as a railroad or highway as they came in toward Bastogne. Several check points were then given to them from the map. When the approaching planes were definitely located, an approach direction was given that would bring them straight in over the target. This procedure eliminated all need for circling and searching and helped them surprise the enemy. When the bombs and gun ammunition were expended, the planes were ordered up to a safe altitude to patrol the perimeter of the defenses or were given specific reconnaissance missions. Their reconnaissance reports were used as the basis for giving targets for succeeding flights and for giving the ground forces advance information on the build-up of enemy strength. After the first flight there were always targets listed ahead. Captain Parker, carefully monitoring the air, also came across flights assigned to other ground forces battling in the Bulge which had no missions for their bombs. He would then call to them and he often succeeded in persuading them to drop their bombs in the Bastogne area. In a few minutes these planes would be back on their assigned missions.

During the first four days of their support, December 23 to 26, the planes averaged more than 250 sorties daily. After that there were two days of bad weather and then the weather came fair again. But it was on December 23 that the air support clanged the bell most loudly and thereby assured decision for the American forces. Colonel Roberts, watching the planes at work, said with enthusiasm that the effect was worth two or three infantry divisions. General McAuliffe bracketed their work with the overwhelming superiority of his artillery and the supreme courage of the men on the ground in his analysis of why Bastogne was saved.

It was not unusual during the siege to have an infantryman call in that five tanks were coming at him and then see six P-47s diving at the tanks within 20 minutes.

19. WEST OF BASTOGNE

FOR SIX DAYS the enemy had made only a few swift passes at General McAuliffe's line facing toward the west. That was the way the command and staff had figured the battle was most likely to develop. Colonel Kinnard, who had worked out the tactical plan for the defense of Bastogne, felt that the forces could be spread thinnest toward the southwest.

Between Colonel Harper, commanding the 327th, and Lieutenant Colonel Ray C. Allen, commanding the 3d Battalion which held the attenuated lines covering toward Neufchâteau, there passed a jest typifying the situation. "How are you doing on your left?" "Good! We have two jeeps out there."

In the northwest sector, the Germans accommodated General McAuliffe's plan of saving the 502d Parachute Infantry for his Sunday punch and that regiment had relatively little fighting though it went through a great many motions.

In the beginning Colonel Allen's 3d Battalion, 327th, became engaged because of the enemy penetration which on the night of December 19-20 reached the Bois de Herbaimont from the direction of Houffalize and overran and captured the 326th Medical Company near crossroads "X." Nine men from the 28th Division - remnant of a group of more than 100 men - got back to Colonel Allen's command post at 2030 and told him how this same German force had ambushed and destroyed their company. It was the first information that the Bastogne-St. Hubert road had been cut and it meant the probable end of any possibility that supplies could be brought in from the northwest. The 101st Division Headquarters became alarmed. At 2200 Colonel Allen was told to move a company out against the roadblock which the enemy had established and destroy it.

Company B under Captain Robert J. McDonald was two hours in preparing for the attack, but it moved out at midnight, December 20-21, and was approaching the roadblock after about a 90-minute march. The men moved down the ditches on either side of the St. Hubert road with two guides walking on the road to keep contact in the darkness. Ahead, they could see a number of vehicles burning and they could hear the enemy laughing and talking. The horns on several of the vehicles had become stuck, adding volume to the sounds which guided them toward their target. The company moved to a ridge within 75 yards of the roadblock, and there deployed. The din from the German position was such that they accomplished this movement without

Men on guard in a pine plantation near Bastogne.

being detected. They formed up with the 2d Platoon on the left, the 3d Platoon on the right, and the 1st Platoon in the center, supported by the heavier weapons. One squad of the 2d Platoon moved to the Sprimont road and formed a block across it about 100 yards from crossroads "X" On the other flank a squad from the 3d Platoon established a block for the same purpose about 100 yards outside the enemy outposts.

Captain McDonald had figured that the roadblock on the right would take longest to establish, so he directed the squad leader to fire two quick rifle shots when his men were in position. The plan worked perfectly. When the two shots were fired, the center moved forward, the men shooting from the hip as they advanced. The Germans were taken wholly by surprise and most of them fled toward the Bois de Herbaimont just to the north whence they had come originally. So doing, they crossed the killing ground which was covered by the squad on the right under Technical Sergeant Mike Campano. They were in such numbers that Campano's men could hardly shoot fast enough. More than 50 Germans were killed. None was taken prisoner. Company B didn't lose a man.

When the last German had been cleared from the area roadblocks were organized in all directions, with an especially strong block being set up on the highway to Salle (31 miles southwest of Bertogne). In this general position, Company B became the farthest outpost of the division. In their search of the area the company found three Americans who had been prisoners of the Germans. One was a Negro truck driver and the other two were from the Finance Department of the 28th Division. They also found two dead paratroopers whose throats had been slashed; they guessed that these men had been patients when the hospital was overrun. A number of American trucks were recovered, some containing medical supplies, one carrying a load of mail and another loaded with explosives.

On finding an American light tank among the enemy booty,

Company B incorporated it into their defenses along with several caliber .50 machine guns from the recaptured trucks. The noise of the skirmish had drawn an artillery observer from the 333d Field Artillery Group and he attached himself to Company B and stood ready to deliver supporting fire from the 155mm. howitzers when it would be needed.

At 0700 on December 21 an enemy column was seen approaching from the direction of Salle. The men at the roadblock guessed it was an artillery battery for it contained nine half-tracks, seven 75mm. guns and seven light vehicles. Captain McDonald's men were in a cut above the highway and their position was so well screened that the German column came to within 25 yards before the defenders opened fire. Then they let them have it with all weapons-their rifles, machine guns, a 57mm. gun and the guns of the light tank. Only one light vehicle from the column managed to turn and get away. All of the enemy guns were captured intact but they could not be moved to town and they were therefore destroyed with the aid of the recaptured explosives.

Shortly thereafter, two tanks supported by a group of German infantry tried to flank the position from the northwest. Company B crippled one tank with a rocket and the other tank withdrew. The infantry group was driven back by small-arms fire from Company B's position, supported by artillery fire.

At noon the roadblock positions were put under fire by enemy tanks operating to the southward of Salle. The tank fire was silenced by two tank destroyers from the 705th Tank Destroyer Battalion which had just come forward to help Captain McDonald's company. However, by this time it had become clear that the roadblock had little importance. Patrols had been sent out to the northwest and southwest and they returned with information that the highway bridges in both directions had been blown. Since the highway was of no further service as a supply route for the Division, Company B was ordered to return to the battalion sector. It did so in the early evening.

At 0900 on December 22, one German group cut the road to Mont southeast of Flamizoulle. (Near Mande-St.-Étienne.) The outpost which sighted it said that it had set up a roadblock with "two half-tracks, one jeep and a trailer." Just before noon, Colonel Allen put on an attack directly south to clear the road. He took twenty-five prisoners and drove the rest off. The motor vehicles turned out to be ordinary farm carts which the Germans had hooked together for use as a block. A platoon of Colonel Templeton's tank destroyers then reconnoitered the road, the sections covering one another alternately from one terrain feature to the next. They reported to Colonel Allen that the road was open.

In the northwest sector, the 502d Parachute Infantry engaged directly without any long-range sparring with the enemy. That came of the order which initially took Colonel Stopka's 3d Battalion, 502d, to Recogne to help extricate the Noville force (See Chapter 7). Four tank destroyers accompanied the battalion to Recogne and stayed there, backing up the line. They got no action the first day though two men and a jeep from the 705th's Reconnaissance Company set up as an evacuation team and shuttled the wounded out of the 502d area after a heavy shelling by the German tank artillery.

At 0730 on December 21, the 1st Battalion, 502d, moved to the area just east of Grosse-Hez (two miles east of Champs) on Division order, and with this shifting of the line, Company A was ordered back to its own battalion. (It had been attached to the 2d Battalion to fill out the 2d's long front.) One hour later, the 1st Battalion started up the road toward Recogne. Company G of the 506th Parachute Infantry bad been hit at Foy and had pulled back its left flank to high ground. This maneuver exposed Colonel Stopka's (2d Battalion) right flank which was anchored in the first few buildings at the north end of Recogne. Stopka had already swung his reserve, Company G, around to his right and faced it south so as to cover the open flank. He bad been helped a little by one of the tank destroyers. The morning was intensely foggy and enemy armor could be beard roaming around just beyond the murk. Sergeant Lazar Hovland got a clear sight of one enemy tank and set it afire in four rounds. A second German tank fired on Hovland and missed; Hovland crippled it with a quick shot but it pulled back into the fog.

By the new order from 101st Division, the 1st Battalion was to clean out Recogne finally and then fill the gap between the 502d and 506th regiments. The order was changed a few minutes later when Colonel Sink (506th commander) reported to General McAuliffe that despite Company G's difficulty the 506th's position was pretty sound. General McAuliffe decided that it made little difference whether he held Recogne. The 1st Battalion, 502d, which had been sweeping forward with two companies abreast, was told to keep on moving but in column of companies. General McAuliffe asked Colonel Stopka if he could disengage, pull back of Recogne and stand on a line running southeastward to where he could join Colonel Sink's flank. Inasmuch as Company G was already standing on this line which curved crescent-fashion around a reverse slope, Stopka said he would be glad to make the move. At noontime the 1st Battalion was moved back to Grosse-Hez and Company A was moved to the south of Longchamps to stop anything that might come that way. The 377th Field Artillery Battalion had given support to the 502d during the latter stage of this operation and had fired 60 rounds on the highway from Salle to Bertogne. The fire knocked out six vehicles of a German column which was turned back by these losses.

On December 22 the enemy build-up along the Salle-Bertogne road continued at such a pace that at noontime Colonel Chappuis, the 502d's commander, moved Company A to Champs and the rest of the 1st Battalion to Hemroulle (two miles west of Bastogne), which faced them to the westward. A platoon from Company B was set up as a roadblock, where Company A had been, along the Longchamps-Bastogne road.

The 3d Battalion received German probing attacks all day long, but on a limited scale. Two of the tank destroyers which had been with Colonel Stopka's 3d Battalion were switched over to support Company A in Champs. A patrol was sent to Rouette, a mile north of Champs, to check on enemy activities. It encountered a small detachment of Germans in the village, engaged 14 of them in a 20-minute fight, drove them off with machine-gun and rifle fire and withdrew under cover of fire from the 377th Parachute FA Battalion.

On December 23, the positions were unchanged. Another patrol went into Rouette under the leadership of First Lieutenant David E. White. They got close enough to see that the enemy was occupying a line of outposts on high ground which overlooked the roads to Champs and Givry (two miles northwest of Champs). The enemy was feverishly at work setting up roadblocks of farm carts bound together. There was a great deal of digging going on next to the positions.

Farther to the southward the signs were becoming equally ominous. Colonel Allen's 3d Battalion of the 327th Glider Infantry was situated in defense of the area of Flamierge, Flamizoulle and the St. Hubert highway west of Mande-St.-Étienne. This put it well to the west of any other unit, without friendly contact on either its right or left. Feeling that his battalion was overextended, Colonel Allen issued a withdrawal plan to his units on December 21 which was known as Plan A. By this plan, Company C would move through Company B in Flamizoulle and Company B would then follow and go through Company A. It was the responsibility of Company A to hold off the enemy until the two other companies were situated on the high ground west of Champs and Grandes-Fanges (a mile to the south). Company A would then withdraw through Company B and Company C would go into a reserve position.

At noon on December 23, patrols reported enemy tanks approaching from the woods to the south of the St. Hubert road. On drawing nearer, this force revealed itself as twelve tanks accompanied by infantry in snow suits. About 1330 Colonel Allen's outposts began their withdrawal without trying to engage the German armor. Allen was fearful that the Germans would move to his right and cut him off from Bastogne. Instead, they moved to the left and halted on the ridge just south of the main road near Cochleval. From this ground they fired upon Company Cs position, but upon trying to advance, were turned back by the American artillery. In one sortie they lost two tanks to artillery fire and the rest of the German armor then withdrew to turret defilade and continued to fire into Company C for the rest of the afternoon. Six of Colonel Templeton's tank destroyers (of the 705th), along with the reconnaissance platoon, had been in position where with good fortune they might have supported Company C in the first stage of this action. But as they pulled out of the cut just beyond Mande-St.-Étienne, enemy tanks shelled them from the woods off their flank and two tank destroyers were lost immediately. This caused a more cautious attitude on the part of the other tank destroyers and they withdrew slightly while the reconnaissance platoon went forward to screen them on the left flank. The other tank destroyers distributed themselves so as to block the roads leading into Mont and the reconnaissance Platoon dug in along the same line.

As darkness came on, Colonel Allen got word that his roadblock at Flamierge had been overrun by an enemy infantry force wearing snow suits. This German column had come down the St. Hubert highway from out of the northwest. Allen's men had been under the mistaken impression that a friendly force - the 4th Armored Division - would arrive by this same route. They mistook the identity of the group and let it come on until the time had passed for successful resistance.

Four tanks moving along with the road column suddenly opened fire on Company C, hitting a number of men and destroying the company aid station, an antitank gun and a pile of mortar ammunition with the first few rounds. The four tanks pressed on against the company position. At the same time the ten tanks to the southward began coming over the ridge. Company C withdrew as best it could.

Colonel Allen figured that by now his whole battalion position was in jeopardy and he ordered Plan A put into effect, But Company C was in such confusion that it couldn't carry out the withdrawal exactly as planned. One platoon got out to the southeastward by way of the main road to escape being cut off. The other platoons pulled back along the predetermined route. Company B came through Company A as planned and took position on the left flank of the high ground where Colonel Allen had determined to make his stand. Company A moved to the rear in reserve. However, Company C's losses were such that Company A had to come back forward again and take Company C's place in the line. Fortunately, the enemy did not press the attack.

Allen told his men, "This is our last withdrawal. Live or die - this is it."

He had spoken correctly; the battalion was never pushed from that ground though it was still to face its worst ordeal.

The next day was quiet. The men cleaned their weapons and waited for Christmas Eve.

20. CHRISTMAS EVE

CHRISTMAS EVE WAS quiet. The commanders and staffs took official notice of the occasion. To all of the command posts within Bastogne went a G-2 reminder from the 101st's chief joker, Colonel Danahy. It was a sitrep overlay in red, white and green, the red outlining the enemy positions completely encircling the town and the green showing only in the words "Merry Christmas" across the position held by the defenders.

General McAuliffe also rose to the occasion with an inspired communiqué in which he told his men about the German demand for surrender and his answer to them. The rest of his Christmas message read as follows:

What's merry about all this, you ask? We're fighting - it's

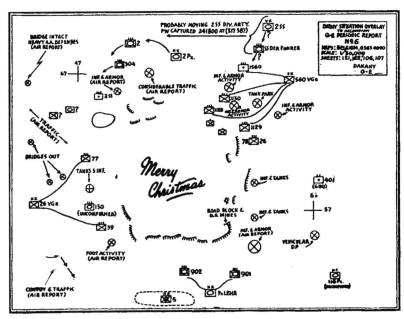

Map 18: Christmas Eve at Bastogne

German propaganda leaflet (two sides) fired by artillery shell into the American lines on Christmas Eve.

cold - we aren't home. All true, but what has the proud Eagle Division accomplished with its worthy comrades of the 10th Armored Division, the 705th Tank Destroyer Battalion and all the rest? Just this: We have stopped cold everything that has been thrown at us from the north, east, south and west. We have identifications from four German panzer divisions, two German infantry divisions and one German parachute division. These units, spearheading the last desperate German lunge, were heading straight west for key points when the Eagle Division was hurriedly ordered to stem the advance. How effectively this was done will be written in history; not alone in our Division's glorious history but in world history. The Germans actually did surround us, their radios blared our doom. Allied troops are counterattacking in force. We continue to hold Bastogne. By holding Bastogne we assure the success of the Allied armies. We know that our Division commander, General Taylor, will say: "Well done!" We are giving our country and our loved ones at home a worthy Christmas present and being privileged to take part in this gallant feat of arms are truly making for ourselves a merry Christmas.

Privately, on the phone that night to General Middleton, McAuliffe expressed his true feeling about Christmas in these words: "The finest Christmas present the 101st could get would be a relief tomorrow."

But General McAuliffe's greeting to his troops proved to be in every part a prophetic utterance though the quiet of Christmas Eve did not last for long.

That night the town was bombed twice. During the first raid, in the late evening, a bomb landed on the hospital of the 20th Armored Infantry Battalion near the intersection of the main roads from Arlon and Neufchâteau. It caved in the roof, burying 20 patients and killing a Belgian woman who was serving as a nurse. Another bomb landed on the headquarters of Combat Command B, doing heavy damage and knocking down the Christmas tree in the message center. The men set up the tree

Map 19

again, and in an elaborate ceremony, one of the sergeants pinned the Purple Heart on a mangled doll.

Except for those bombings Christmas Eve passed without unusual pressure from the enemy. The journal entries of the different regiments all use the word "quiet" in describing the period. But that is a word that simply does not record the tumult in the thoughts and emotions of the men of Bastogne. Such was their reaction to the Christmas and to the memories surrounding it, that for the first time all around the perimeter men felt fearful. It seemed to them that the end was at hand. That night many of them shook hands with their comrades. They said to one another that it would probably be their last night together. Many of the commanders saw this happening, though they knew it had little relation to the still strong tactical situation. *[Colonel Ewell, among other commanders, commented on this in the second interview. Many of the men spoke of how fearful they felt on Christmas Eve.]*

In the 502d Parachute Infantry the officers heard Christmas Eve Mass in the tenth-century chapel of the beautiful Rolle Château which they were using for a command post." It was a

The château at Rolle, 502d Parachute Infantry Command Post

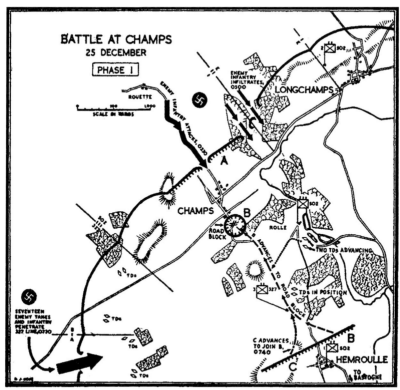

Map 20

happy occasion, well attended by the neighboring Belgians who had rounded out the regimental messes with contributions of flour and sides of beef from their own stores.

The regimental officers turned in about 0130 on Christmas morning.

At 0245 there was an intense shelling of the forward area by the German artillery. Lieut. Colonel Patrick J. Cassidy, the 502d's executive officer, called Captain Wallace A. Swanson of Company A who reported that his front had suddenly become active (see map 20). But he added that the situation was obscure; he could not figure out yet what the Germans intended.

At 0330 Colonel Cassidy called Captain Swanson again. Swanson said that the enemy was on top of him. While they were talking, the line went out. Colonel Cassidy awakened Colonel Chappuis, the regimental commander. Then all lines went out.

Chappuis called his 1st Battalion by radio and told them to get ready to move, adding that the commander, Major John D. Hanlon, was to come to Rolle as quickly as possible. By radio Chappuis heard from Swanson that Germans in large numbers were in Champs and that his men were locked in a hand-to-hand and house-to-house fight with them. Major Hanlon reported at the command post and was told by Colonel Chappuis to move Company B to the Champs road just west of Rolle and then get forward into Champs and help Captain Swanson's Company A.

While Swanson was becoming engaged, other German forces had filtered through the woods to the east of Champs on the 2d Battalion's left flank. After reporting this to regiment, Lieut. Colonel Thomas H. Sutliffe, the 2d Battalion commander, shifted part of his force leftward against this threat. Colonel Chappuis supported his move by instructing Major Hanlon to send one platoon of Company B to the right to join hands with Company E. Hanlon called in at 054512 and said the Germans were still fighting in Champs. He did not want to put the rest of his battalion into the village until it became light because the darkness and confusion were so bad that it was almost impossible to distinguish friend from enemy. Colonel Chappuis told him to hold steady.

As Chappuis and Cassidy estimated the situation at 502d Headquarters, Company B was already backing up Company A and would still be effective if Champs were lost, whereas it might lose its reserve value if it pushed on into the village and the Germans came around it. So they waited. They knew that somewhere a real blow was coming but they could not figure where. So far the German pressure had jarred them only at the right and center of the 502d and was coming at them from the north. They looked anxiously to the westward where their sector joined that of the 327th Glider Infantry. Their command post was under heavy artillery fire and was no longer in either telephone or radio communication with Headquarters, 101st

Bazooka position in the 502d Parachute Infantry area. It was over this terrain on Christmas Day that enemy tanks moved on Rolle. The enemy tank in the foreground was destroyed in that fight.

Division.

Just as the first light of Christmas morning broke, the S-2 of the 1st Battalion, First Lieutenant Samuel B. Nickels, Jr., came at a dead run into the château where the Headquarters, 502d, was. "There are seven enemy tanks and lots of infantry coming over the hill on your left," he said. He had first sighted them moving along parallel to the ridge southwest of Hemroulle. They were striking toward the ground where the 502d and 327th joined hands.

The Rolle Château was emptied almost before Lieutenant Nickels had finished speaking. Cooks, clerks, radio men and the chaplains collected under Captain James C. Stone, the 502d headquarters commandant, and rushed west to the next hill.18 From the château gate at Rolle, the road dips down through a deep swale then rises onto the ridge where it joins the main road into Hemroulle, about two miles northwest of Bastogne. The road line is on high ground all the way until just before it reaches Hemroulle where it drops down again to the village.19 Captain Stone's scratch headquarters force ran across the swale and took up firing positions close to the road and facing westward. Within a few minutes they were joined by the men of the regiment's wounded who were able to walk. Major Douglas T. Davidson, the regimental surgeon of the 502d, had run to the chateau stable that was serving as a temporary hospital, rallied his patients, handed them rifles and then led them out against the tanks.

They could see the tanks coming on toward them now. From the archway of Rolle Château it was about 600 yards to the first line of German armor. Colonels Chappuis and Cassidy and the radio operator looked westward from the archway and could see just the outline of the enemy movement in the dim light. They were now the only men at the headquarters.

Colonel Cassidy called Major Hanlon and told him to leave Company B where it was but to get the company ready to protect its own rear and then try to get Company C faced to the west to

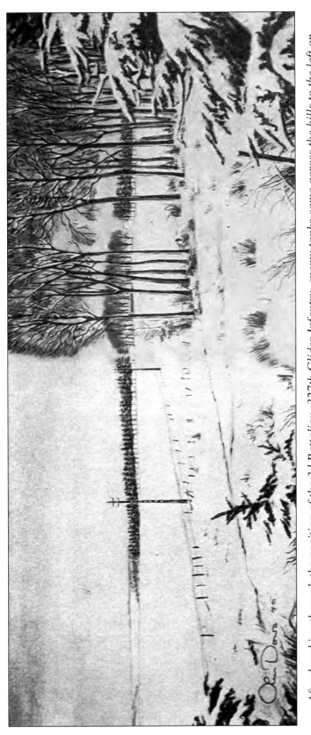

After breaking through the position of the 3d Battalion, 327th Glider Infantry, enemy tanks came across the hills to the left on Christmas Day to attack Champs and Rolle. The road leading to the right goes to Champs. Paralleling the second row of trees a road goes to Rolle. Company C, 502d Parachute Infantry was attacked while marching along the center road. It then fell back to join some tank destroyers of the 705th Tank Destroyer Battalion at the trees in the foreground. From this position many enemy tanks were destroyed.

meet the German tanks as they came on.

The 327th Glider Infantry was already engaged. At 0500 Colonel Harper had heard by phone from Company A of his 3d Battalion that 18 enemy tanks were formed for attack just east of Mande-St.-Étienne. At 0710 the German armor supported by infantry of the 77th Grenadier Regiment smashed through the positions held by Companies A and B. In coming through the companies, the tanks fired all their guns and the German infantrymen riding the tanks blazed away with their rifles. The spearpoint of the German armor had already broken clear through to the battalion command post. At the 327th regimental headquarters Colonel Harper heard by telephone of the breakthrough, and on the heels of that message came word from Lieut. Colonel Cooper that his 463d Parachute Field Artillery Battalion already had the German tanks under fire. At 0715 Colonel Allen, the 3d Battalion (327th) commander, called and said that the tanks were right on him.

Harper asked, "How close?"

"Right here!" answered Allen. "They are firing point-blank at me from 150 yards range. My units are still in position but I've got to run." But Colonel Allen's battalion had not been wholly taken by surprise. "Tanks are coming toward you!" Captain Preston E. Towns, commanding Company C, had telephoned to Allen.

"Where?" Allen had asked.

"If you look out your window now," said Captain Towns, "you'll be looking right down the muzzle of an 88."

Christmas Day was just then breaking. Colonel Allen stayed at his 3d Battalion, 327th, command post only long enough to look out of his window, and prove what Towns had told him, and to call Colonel Harper and tell him he was getting out. Then he ran as fast as he could go and the German tanker fired at him as he sprinted toward the woods. He could see the muzzle blasts over his shoulder in the semidarkness. But all of the shots were

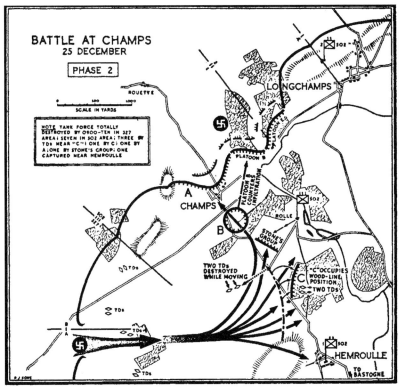

Map 21

leading him. The Germans were giving him credit for more speed than his legs possessed.

Two members of Allen's staff followed him. As they all came out of the other end of the woods, men of Colonel Chappuis' 502d Parachute Infantry along the ridge road saw them and promptly pinned them down with heavy rifle fire. The three then crawled back to the woods, circled south through a little valley and returned to Hemroulle.

As they came out of the woods the second time, they were fired on by artillerymen of Colonel Cooper's 463d Parachute Field Artillery Battalion who had formed a skirmish line in case the enemy broke through the infantry. But Colonel Allen was getting tired of all this and he waved his handkerchief vigorously until finally the gunners lowered their rifles and let the party come in.

Colonel Harper, on getting the phone call made by Allen just before Allen had to dash from his headquarters, realized that there was now no control over the 3d Battalion, 327th. So he sent his own S-3, Major Jones, with his radio to Colonel Cooper's artillery command post and Jones got there just as Allen did, and he got through at once to the companies with the radio.

In the meantime the forward line had held (see map 21), partly because of the quick thinking of Captain McDonald of Company B. He had heard Colonel Allen's urgent report to Colonel Harper over his own telephone and he at once called Companies A and C by radio. "The battalion commander has had to get out," he said to them. "I can see you from where I am. Your best bet is to stay where you are. Hold tight to your positions and fight back at them."

That was what they did. The main body of the German armor rolled straight through Company A's lines - 18 white-camouflaged tanks moving in column. The men of Company A, 327th (First Lieutenant Howard G. Bowles was the acting commanding officer), stayed in their foxholes and took it, replying with their rifles and whatever other weapons were at hand. After the tide of German steel had passed over and through them, 4 men of the company were dead and 5 lay wounded. But the 68 survivors were up and fighting, and in the next round of the battle they captured 92 German prisoners.

Having crashed through Colonel Harper's 327th front, the German armor split as it came on toward the ridge and half of it swung north toward Rolle where Lieutenant Nickels saw it and warned Colonel Chappuis, commander of the 502d Parachute Infantry, in time for him to make his last-minute preparation. Companies B and C, 502d, were even then in column of twos moving up the road toward Champs.

Thus far Colonel Templeton's 705th Tank Destroyer Battalion had played only a minor part in the defense of the sector, but their best moments were approaching. Two of the tank destroyers had been of some assistance to Captain Swanson (Company A, 502d) in his fight for Champs. They were already in position there when the German attack got under way, one destroyer in the center of Champs and another slightly to the west of it so placed that it could cover the road to the southwest and the ridge to the north and northwest. Upon setting up, the tank destroyer crews manned four machine guns on the ground around their centrally located guns. This position held when the German infantry closed on Champs and the tank destroyer force even spared a few of its men to go forward and help the paratroopers root the enemy out of the houses.

Too, the heavy guns were used for close-up interdiction fire to keep the enemy from moving any deeper into the village. In this work, the 37mm. guns, firing canister, were especially effective. Captain Swanson got one of the tank destroyers, under Sergeant Lawrence Valletta, to go forward and blast a house where about thirty Germans had taken cover. Sergeant Valletta moved right in next to the building, trained his big gun on the doors and windows and blew the place apart. He then shelled two more houses and returned to his original position. Just about dawn, he made a second sortie of the same kind.

To the southward of Champs where the crisis of the Christmas action was swiftly maturing, the tank destroyers got away to a bad start but then staged a swift recovery.35 Two of them from Company B, 705th Battalion, had been in the 327th Glider Infantry area and were out along the road which runs from Rolle toward Grandes-Fanges, a mile to the southwest (this put them to the southward of Company C, 502d Parachute Infantry), when the German attack came over the hill. The crews had at first put their tank destroyers into concealment behind a haystack and from there had engaged the enemy armor at a distance, knocking out two or three tanks. Yet as the power of the German armor became more obvious, they decided to withdraw. That was how it happened that they were moving back toward Rolle and were directly in line with the German tank fire when Company C of the 502d Parachute Infantry faced toward the enemy.

Both tank destroyers were knocked out almost instantly. The men of Company C saw them reel and stop from the enemy fire and realized that the loss of the tank destroyers had helped spare them the worst part of the blow.

The encounter had had one other powerful effect - two tank destroyers from Company C, 705th, were waiting in the woods behind Colonel Chappuis' 502d infantrymen. The German armor, confident that it was now in full command of the field, came on boldly against the infantry line. Colonel Cassidy (executive of the 502d) had sent a runner sprinting toward the woods to alert the two concealed tank destroyers. The runner had been told to run from the guns on to Captain George R. Cody's Company C, 502d, position and tell him that the tank destroyers would be backing him up. But he didn't get there in time.

The guns of the seven Mark IVs were already firing into Company C. About 15 to 20 German infantrymen were riding on the outside of each tank, some firing their rifles. But the

Typical Ardennes countryside between Bastogne and Wiltz.

ground fog was bad and their fire was erratic. Captain Cody turned his men about and told them to fall back to the edge of the forest. Without any part of its line breaking into a general dash for the rear, Company C fell back to the shelter of the trees and there took up positions and opened fire on the tanks with machine guns, bazookas, and rifles. Despite the surprise of the German assault, this movement was carried out with little loss and no disorder.

Then swiftly, there was a complete turning of the situation as Company C's first volleys from its new position took toll of the German infantry clinging to the tanks. Dead and wounded pitched from the vehicles into the snow. As if with the purpose of saving their infantry, the tanks veered left toward Champs and the position held by Company B, 502d.

Until this moment the two tank destroyers in the woods behind Company C had not fired a round. *[Colonels Chappuis and Cassidy were in a position to observe the relationship in time of the tank destroyer fire to the rest of the action.]* But as the tank line pivoted and began to move northward along the top of the ridge, the flank the German armor became completely exposed and the two tank destroyers went into action. *[The tank destroyer account of this episode is not well rounded out but the crew were not in position to see the action clearly.]* So did Company B, which was now firing at the enemy front. Three of the Mark IVs were hit and knocked out by the tank destroyer fire before they completed their turning movement. One was stopped by a bazooka round from Company C. A fifth tank was hit and stopped by a rocket from Captain Stone's scratch group from Headquarters, 502d. *[This is 502d Parachute Infantry's report of the detail. The tank destroyers themselves claim credit for a greater number of hits.]* The infantry riding on the tanks were cut to pieces by bullet fire. As Company C s part of the battle ended there were 67 German dead and 35 prisoners, many of them wounded, in the area around the ruined tanks.

One tank did break through Company B and charge on into Champs. Company A, 502d, fired bazookas at it and it was also shelled by a 57mm. gun which had taken position in the village. The tank was hit by both types of fire but which weapon made the kill is uncertain.

Captain James J. Hatch, S-3 of the 502d, had gone forward to reconnoiter Company A's situation and was in the Company A command post at the time. He heard the fight going on outside, grabbed his pistol and opened the door. He was looking straight into the mouth of the tank's 75mm. gun at a range of 15 yards.

Hatch closed the door and said to the others, "This is no place for my pistol."

The seventh tank in the German group - it was later determined that this was the same tank that had knocked out the two tank destroyers - was captured intact at Hemroulle. By 0900, December 25, the action was cleared up around Rolle. Headquarters of the 502d Parachute Infantry had called 101st Division Headquarters and asked about the situation of 327th Glider Infantry over on its left. Colonel Kinnard (101st Airborne Division G-3) reported that the 327th's lines were generally intact and the situation there well in hand.

In the 327th's sector there had been four tank destroyers behind Captain McDonald's Company B and four behind Lieutenant Bowles' Company A. Captain Towns' Company C was unsupported by tank destroyers but Colonel Harper had sent him two Sherman tanks on hearing that the German attack was coming.

These guns, the bazooka fire of the 327th Glider Infantry outfits and the barrage fire of Colonel Cooper's 463d Parachute Field Artillery Battalion had dealt in detail with that part of the German armor that tried to ride on through toward Hemroulle after breaking Harper's front. The German tanks were fired at from so many directions and with such a mixture of fire that it was not possible to see or say how each tank met its doom. One

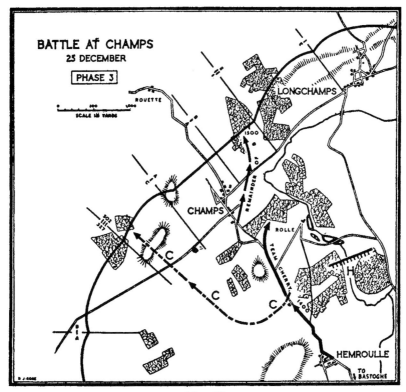

Map 22

battery from the 463d stopped two tanks at a range of 600 yards and then some men ran out from the battery position and captured the crews. Eighteen German tanks had been seen on that part of the 327th Glider Infantry's front that morning. Eighteen tanks had driven on through the infantry. But not one got away. When the fighting died at last there were eighteen disabled German tanks, many of them with fire-blackened hulls, scattered out through the American positions along the ridges running from Hemroulle to Champs.

In the 502d Parachute Infantry area, the wire maintenance men had kept on working right through the fire fight and by 0900 the lines were again in solid.58 None of the German infantry had managed an escape.

The few survivors, upon recoiling, were rounded up by the members of Colonel Allen's overrun 3d Battalion, 327th. The

Map 23

German tankers died inside their tanks.

Although Company C, 502d, had been compelled to engage without artillery support because of the closeness of the action, its losses were negligible. It was put in position along the high ground west of the scene of the skirmish. At about the same time the Company C fight ended, Company A, 502d, was getting Champs under control and was doing the last of its rat hunting through the village houses. Company B was put over to the eastward of Company A to fill out the line as far as the 3d Battalion. In getting to this position, Company B, 502d, took heavy losses from enemy artillery while moving across the high ground north of Champs, but by 1500 the position was complete (see map 22). Company A counted 98 Germans killed and 79 enlisted men and 2 officers captured in the Champs action.

About 0800 on Christmas, 101st Division moved Force

Cherry out through Hemroulle to a position on the high ground along the edge of the woods to the southward of the 502d Parachute Infantry. Colonel Cherry stayed there until after dark to cover the restoration of the 1st Battalion, 327th, position. He then pulled back to Hemroulle. A German field order captured during the morning fight showed that the German tank and infantry mission that came to grief along the ridge south and west of Rolle had been attempted by the 115th Panzergrenadier Regiment of the 15th Panzergrenadier Division (see map 23). Two battalions of the 77th Panzergrenadier Regiment, supported by the division artillery of the 26th Volksgrenadier Division, had implemented the assault against Champs and to the southward which preceded the Panzer advance.

Christmas day closed with Colonel Chappuis and Colonel Cassidy of the 502d sitting down to a table spread with a can of sardines and a box of crackers. *[This was the high tide of the German attack against the 502d Parachute Infantry. The 1st Battalion, 502d, was again attacked and on December 27 was driven off the hill briefly. By that time Division had been joined by the force from the south. During December 26, the 502d continued to maintain an all-around defense of the position. Six prisoners were taken near Champs.]*

General McAuliffe, disappointed that no relief force had come, called General Middleton and said, "We have been let down."

21. THE RELIEF

O N THE MORNING of December 26, the German forces renewed their pressure against the western side of the Bastogne perimeter (see map 24). But they did not press their attack in real strength and the American lines held solid. Around the other parts of the defending circle, the day was relatively quiet though both sides intensified their air activity.

The intervention of the air directly hastened the hour when the enemy encirclement of Bastogne was broken through by the arrival of the armored column from the south. Since 0600 on December 22, the three Combat Commands of the 4th Armored Division had been fighting their way steadily toward Bastogne by three separate routes from their assembly areas north of Arlon. They had met intense resistance all the way along the line and had taken heavy losses in men and tanks. By 1500 on December 26, Combat Command Reserve of the 4th had arrived at the high ground overlooking Clochimont and was preparing to attack toward the village of Sibret. This put the command about four miles to the southwestward of Bastogne with their local objective about one mile to their own northwestward. As the attack was about to get under way, the men saw and heard what seemed to be "hundreds" of C-47 planes coming directly over them and bound for Bastogne. The spectacle encouraged Lieutenant Colonel Creighton W. Abrams, Jr., commanding the 37th Tank Battalion, and Lieutenant Colonel George L. Jaques, commanding the 53d Armored Infantry Battalion, to make a break for Bastogne, disregarding their original mission. They believed that Sibret was strongly held. Colonel Abrams' force had been cut down to twenty medium tanks and Colonel Jaques' force was short 230 men. They figured that it might cost less to ignore Sibret and attack straight toward Bastogne.

At 1520, December 26, Colonel Abrams ordered his S-3, Captain William A. Dwight, to take a light team composed of tanks and infantry, break northeast to the village of Assenois and keep moving until he reached the Bastogne lines. The artillery with Combat Command Reserve, 4th Armored Division - three battalions of 105mm. and one battery of 155mm. howitzers - was directed to stand ready to place a concentration on Assenois as the team moved up to it. Such was the plan.

In the execution of it, the commander of the leading tank called for artillery support as soon as he came within sight of the village. The guns poured ten rounds apiece against the target, concentrating their fire against the woods north of town and into an area in the southern edge of town where the enemy was supposed to be strongly fixed with antitank guns. Combat

Map 24

Command Reserve's shells were still dropping on Assenois when the first tanks moved in among the houses. There were some infantry losses from our own fire. In the smoke and confusion, the infantry company of Captain Dwight's team dismounted and engaged the enemy in a fight for the village.

But five tanks and one infantry half-track stuck to the letter of their assignment and kept moving toward Bastogne. Three of the tanks had forged several hundred yards to the fore and the enemy strewed Teller mines between them and the rest of the tank force as they were pulling out of Assenois. The half-track hit a mine and was destroyed. Captain Dwight jumped down from his tank to clear the other mines away, so that he could get forward with his two tanks. Meanwhile, the three lead tanks kept going and at 1650 First Lieutenant Charles P. Boggess, commanding officer of Company C, 37th Tank Battalion, drove the first vehicle from the 4th Armored Division to within the lines of the 326th Airborne Engineer Battalion, 101st Division, of the Bastogne forces.

This was the beginning. The German encirclement was now finally broken, though some days would pass before the American lines to the south were again firm and several weeks of fighting would ensue before the siege of Bastogne was finally lifted. Captain Dwight, having followed Lieutenant Boggess on into Bastogne, radioed Colonel Abrams to come up with the rest of the breakthrough team.

With them came Major General Maxwell D. Taylor, commander of the 101st Division, who had flown back from the United States to join his Division. General Taylor had arrived in time to lead his men through their bitterest days of fighting on the Bastogne ground, the days yet to come.

Captain Dwight then continued on to report to General McAuliffe and arrange for the convoys to enter the town that night. Assenois was cleared by 2000, December 26, with the capture of 428 prisoners. Before morning, the woods on both

Colonel Danahy, General McAuliffe and Colonel Kinnard.

sides of the road running north from Assenois were cleared sufficiently to assure relatively free use of this line of communication.

Much hard fighting still remained for the other two combat commands of 4th Armored Division before they, too, closed to within the Bastogne perimeter. By their drive north, they had opened an avenue to the south which would insure that the victory won by the Bastogne defenders could be fully exploited

General George S. Patton, Jr., talking with Brigadier General McAuliffe and Lieutentant Colonel Steve A. Chappuis after awarding these officers the Distinguished Service Cross for their actions int the defense of Bastogne.

by the United States Army and the forces of its Allies.

The relief of Bastogne signaled the defeat of the German Army in the Ardennes offensive. But it had cost the 4th Armored Division a price comparable to that exacted from the defenders of Bastogne themselves.2 In the seven days during which its forces were moving to the relief of Bastogne the Division lost about 1,000 men. Its total medium tank strength at the end of the period was equal to the full tank strength of a single battalion.3 As for what this victory - won by the defenders of Bastogne and confirmed by the force that relieved them - availed the Allied cause, and as to how it influenced the emergency of December 1944, there is an official estimate from the command of 12th Army Group.

The After Action Report for December 1944 says:

Preoccupation with the key position of Bastogne dominated enemy strategy to such an extent that it cost him the advantage. of the initiative. The German High Command evidently considered further extension to the west or north as both logistically and strategically unsound without possession of Bastogne, as that town overlooks the main roads and concentration areas of the spearheads. By the end of the month, the all-out effort in the north had become temporarily. defensive; in the west there was a limited withdrawal, and the array of German forces around Bastogne clearly exposed the enemy's anxiety over that position. Until the Bastogne situation is resolved one way or the other no change in strategy can be expected.

How well those words were sustained by the further passage of events is now history.

APPENDIX I. THE CASUALTIES

The casualties of the 101st Airborne Division up to January 6, 1945, in the Bastogne operation were as follows:

	Officers	*Enlisted Men*
Killed	29	312
Wounded	103	1,588
Missing	34	482
	166	2,382

The Artillery losses were extremely light except among forward observers. The Engineer Battalion lost 26 enlisted men and one officer killed and 84 enlisted men wounded up to January 6. Owing to the capture of the hospital, the 326th Medical Company showed the largest number of missing of any unit at Bastogne with 125 gone. There was a surprisingly even distribution of losses among the Infantry regiments:

	327th		501st		502d		506th	
	Off	*EM*	*Off*	*EM*	*Off*	*EM*	*Off*	*EM*
Killed	2	60	68	8	66	5	67	
Wounded	13	279	29	471	22	246	28	359

The total of German prisoners taken was 981. The estimated number of enemy killed is 7,000.

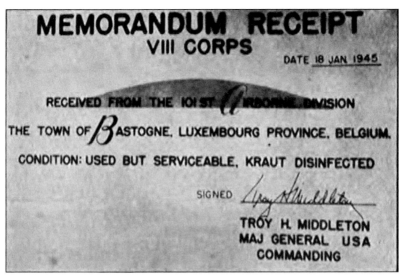

Memorandum receipt given by Major General Troy H. Middleton,
Commanding General of the VIII Corps, to the 101st Airborne Division for
holding Bastogne.

APPENDIX II. THE ENEMY STORY

IN ONE RESPECT, the Bastogne story is complete as told in the preceding chapters. There is the battle as it was seen by the defending forces from within the Bastogne perimeter and as it could be clarified for them by all of the normal and accessible sources of information such as our own official documents, captured enemy documents, interviews with our key personnel at all levels, and interrogation of such of the enemy as fell into our hands in the course of operations. To preserve the integrity of the narrative from the viewpoint of the defenders, it seemed essential that the material be presented in that form. Moreover, since it will be noted in reading this added chapter that the errors caused by so doing were minor indeed, the Bastogne story becomes tangible proof of the competence of our own methods of acquiring intelligence of the enemy and of estimating his capabilities.

There remains, however, the question of exactly what was occurring among the enemy forces while our own forces were defending Bastogne so stoutly. What was their design? How did they view the American action? How did their estimate and judgment of the tactical events modify their own plan and movement?

It has been said in high places that the enemy was not really trying to capture Bastogne. This judgment was taken after a cursory examination of his plan which fell into our hands in the course of the war. But that is not a final truth and if the full importance of all that happened in the first days of the Bastogne defense is to be accurately measured by history, the witnesses must speak from the opposing camp.

In November and December 1945 there took place a series of conferences between the three chief actors in the attack on Bastogne and the author of the Bastogne story. Present were Lieutenant General Heinrich von Lüttwitz, Commanding General of the XXXXVII Panzer Corps, Lieutenant General Fritz Hermann Bayerlein, Commanding General of the Panzer Lehr Division, and Major General Heinz Kokott, Commanding General of the 26th Volksgrenadier Division. Colonel Meinhard von Lauchert, the commander of the 2d Panzer Division, was not present nor was his presence deemed necessary. Of the three divisions, the 2d Panzer had had least to do with the direct attack on Bastogne; and further, the Corps commander, having formerly commanded that division and having a sentimental feeling for it and not too much faith in Von Lauchert, had directly supervised its operation during the German advance. With what at least appeared to be utmost candor, the three enemy commanders proceeded to discuss all that had happened to them.

There were in all ten conferences on these matters, during which the commanders worked with all of the necessary maps and such staff notes as were available to them. Inasmuch as the data on the American operation were already complete, it was easy to provide the check points which would establish the accuracy of their story in all particulars. Colonel H. W. O. Kinnard, who had been G-3 of the 101st Airborne Division during the Bastogne operation, also attended these interrogations. The meeting with Kinnard was a visible shock to the German commanders. It seemed incredible to them that this boyish-faced soldier had been one of their principal antagonists. They asked several times for reassurance on this score. Lüttwitz said, "Are you certain he was chief of operations? Isn't it possible that he was only the chief for one regiment?"

Lüttwitz is an old-time cavalryman. Now past fifty-eight, he is large, gross and paunchy. His monocle and his semi-belligerent manner of speech would suggest that he is the typically arrogant Prussian, but among other German commanders he had the reputation of being especially kind to troops. He would talk only when he had a map before him; then he liked to lay pencils on the map to represent the movements of his regiments. What was most remarkable about him was that in battle he seemed to have concerned himself more with the movements of squads and companies than with the employment of divisions. He was frequently hazy about how his regiments had been disposed but he could invariably say what had been done by a particular patrol or outpost. Once he starts talking, he is extremely windy. He appeared to be chagrined over the fact that he authored the request to Bastogne to surrender; the other commanders concerned all regard that request as a military faux pas. But they believe that Lüttwitz has the "Nuts!" message and that he has hidden it away somewhere as a valuable historical document.

Bayerlein is a short, solidly built man of fifty, sharp-featured and keen of eye. All of his actions are vigorous and his aggressiveness in and out of conversation reminds one of a terrier. This outward seeming hides the fact that he is suffering from a fatal kidney ailment. He prides himself on the fact that in the past ten years he has taught himself to speak English. While working with the American Historical Section, he sat down one evening and wrote as a diversion a fifty-page history of the United States which was quite accurate. His contempt for Lüttwitz is obvious. When Lüttwitz rambles in his conversation, Bayerlein waves a hand in his face and snarls, "Not important! Not important!" He believes that Lüttwitz made the worst fumbles at Bastogne though the record indicates that Bayerlein's individual actions and estimates cost the Corps some of its finest opportunities. About those mistakes and the mistakes of all others, he is brutally frank. They become almost a mania with him. When confronted with his own gross blunders, he puts his head back and laughs with abandon; it seems to be about the one thing that thoroughly amuses him.

Kokott is a shy, scholarly and dignified commander who never raises his voice and appears to be temperate in his actions and judgments. Now past fifty-two, he is doubtless the steadiest man of the three. In his account of battle, he is strictly objective. He shares Bayerlein's opinion of Lüttwitz but is more amused than resentful. Better than any other commander, he saw the true situation at Bastogne though he also made his share of mistakes, as the record shows. He felt, even more strongly than the others, that adherence to the original plan at Bastogne became unwise on December 19 but he is a natural optimist and he expected to win the battle.

The onfall of XXXXVII Panzer Corps against the front held by the American 28th Infantry Division and the general consequences of that onfall have been briefly told in Chapter I of this book. Having made its penetration, the further movements of XXXXVII Corps were intended to be consistent with the overall policy of the Fifth Panzer Army throughout the German Ardennes offensive: The mobile divisions would by-pass points of resistance and remain free to continue the movement; the clearing out of islands of resistance would be done by the slower-moving infantry bodies. The policy of the Army was duly transmitted from Corps down to the divisions. It was believed that the two armored divisions could quickly overrun Bastogne before resistance there could solidify. In their sweep directly westward, the boundary between the 2d Panzer Division on the right and the Panzer Lehr Division on the left, for the attack on Bastogne, was an east-west line about halfway between Bastogne and Noville. The objective of the 2d Panzer Division was the same crossroads X south of the Bois de Herbaimont which figured so prominently in the American story. The purpose of the Panzer Lehr Division was to take Bastogne by attack from the south. This was the original order as established by the initial plan. It was not changed before the battle opened although it was

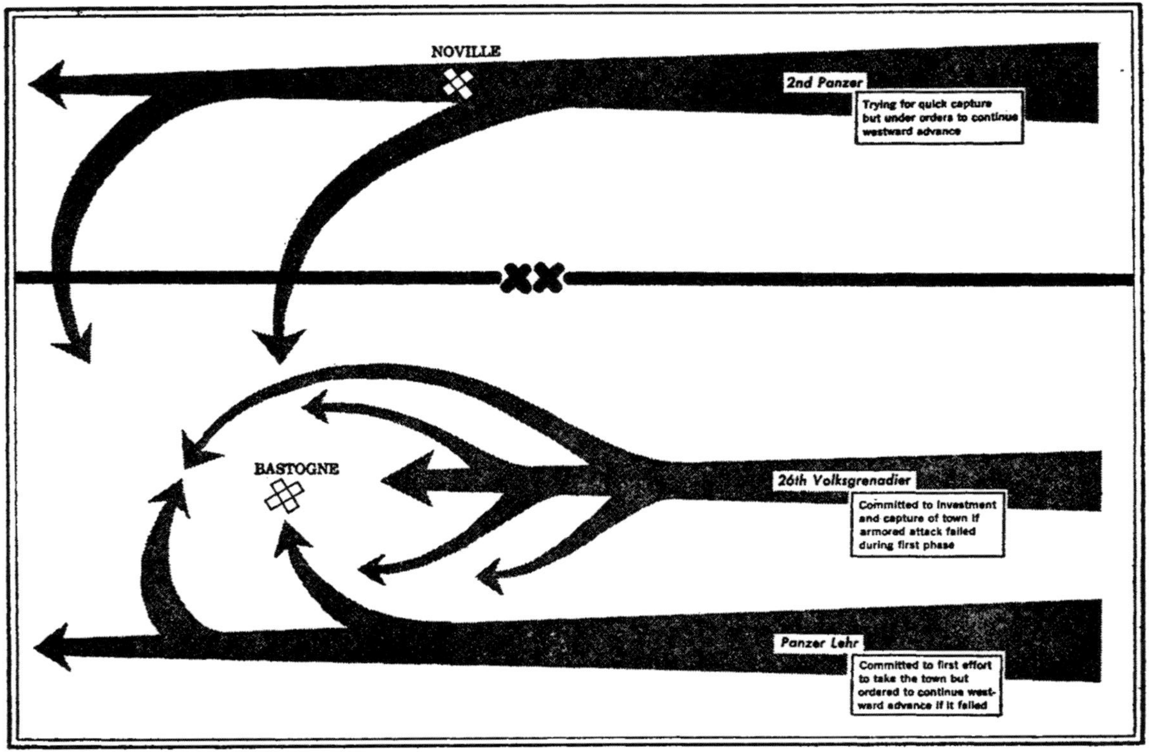

Map 25: Bastogne envelopment according to the German plan

BASTOGNE

NOVILLE

Panzer Lehr
Committed to first effort to take the town but ordered to continue westward advance if it failed

26th Volksgrenadier
Committed to investment and capture of town if armored attack failed during first phase

2nd Panzer
Trying for quick capture but under orders to continue westward advance

in a degree modified.

On December 12, Lüttwitz called his division commanders together, and addressing his remarks especially to Bayerlein, the commander of Panzer Lehr, he said to all of them: "Bastogne must be taken. Otherwise it will remain an abscess on our lines of communication. We must clear out the whole of Bastogne and then march on." He added the instruction that if Bastogne was found to be relatively open, it should be attacked directly by the most feasible route, but that if it were defended in strength frontally, the two armored divisions should attempt to envelop and attack the rear or west. These two expedients failing and quick capture of the town appearing impossible, the two armored divisions were to continue their general advance and the 26th Volksgrenadier Division was to undertake the investment and capture of Bastogne. The effect which this conference produced on the minds of the subordinate commanders is to be measured in the story of their separate actions and decisions.

In the attack of December 16 against the general American front, the Corps attacked with 2d Panzer Division on the right flank and 26th Volksgrenadier Division on the left, and Panzer Lehr Division in reserve. Penetrations into our lines having been made, during December 17 the Panzer Lehr Division moved ahead of the 26th Volksgrenadier (see map 25). On the right, the northern bridgeheads across the Clerf and Our rivers had been built by the 2d Panzer Division; these were the bridgeheads enabling the movement of enemy forces along the road to Longvilly. On the left the engineering units of the 26th Volksgrenadier Division had done the necessary bridging to enable Panzer Lehr to cross the Clerf and Our and push on for Bastogne. The two southern bridgeheads opened onto secondary roads by way of which Panzer Lehr could cut the lines of communication South of Bastogne and attack the town initially from that direction.

The 2d Panzer Division advanced rapidly throughout that day

and the next day. Heavy resistance from our 28th Division units in Clervaux slowed its pace on December 17; but after that there was no check to the progress of the 2d Panzer Division until it came almost to the road intersection to the east of Longvilly, where it intended to veer north and proceed toward Noville.

In mid-afternoon of December 17, Lüttwitz, the XXXXVII Corps commander, visited his front lines where his armor was pushing westward from the bridgeheads. He returned late in the day to his CP near Karlshausen on the east bank of the Our River to find a message from his communications officer lying on his desk. It read that he had intercepted an American radio message saying that the American airborne divisions, then near Reims, had been alerted for a fast movement to the battle area. Lüttwitz looked once more at the map and reasoned that they would be sent to Bastogne.

To Lüttwitz, this spoke volumes. In his own words: "Ever since the Arnhem operation our command had feared another attack by airborne forces. When the message came in, we knew not only that there would be no such attack but that the American Army must be extremely short of reserves in the immediate vicinity. Otherwise, it would not commit airborne divisions of such high standing to the battle." But the knowledge that those forces were bound by ground movement for the same objective as his own forces did not change his plan or his instructions. He was already proceeding toward Bastogne with all possible speed and he calculated that he could get there before our airborne units arrived, and he would be opposed by negligible forces in so doing.

During December 18, the advance continued, with both German armored divisions adhering to the boundaries established in the original plan. Through the day there had been no interruption of progress in either lane that dimmed Lüttwitz's hope of beating the opposing forces into Bastogne. As the night drew on, his divisions were promisingly poised: The forward

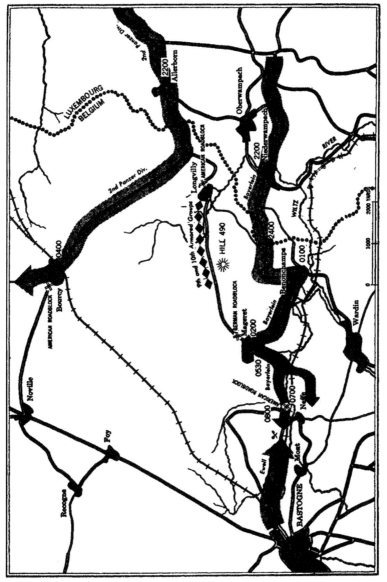

Map 26: Opening German movements: December 18-19

elements of the 2d Panzer were at the point east of Longwilly where the division was to turn north from the main road. The forward elements of Panzer Lehr were at Niederwampach, to the south (see map 26).

It is to be noted that the turning movement of the 2d Panzer Division was taking place at such a distance from the roadblock of our 9th Armored Division in Longvilly (which was in process of being supported and then replaced by the forces under Captain Ryerson of Team Cherry, Combat Command B, 10th Armored Division) that both of these armored bodies could have carried out their assignments without head-on collision. The German force was, of course, turning a shoulder and then exposing a flank toward the American armor in Longvilly; moreover, it was assumed by the German commander that the American armor was in march toward him. He therefore took steps to cover the avenues of approach leading toward his exposed flank. At the same time the Americans in Longvilly, knowing nothing of the turning movement, took it for granted that this German column was coming on down the main road. It was therefore almost inevitable that the two forces would engage but the extent of engagement was limited by the mutually exclusive character of their separate missions.

Panzer Lehr, however, was under no such restriction, since Bastogne lay within its boundary. It was only a question of which was the most opportune road and hour, whether time was left to go directly at the town or whether it was the better part of wisdom to strike first at the lines of communication leading south. To do the former, Bayerlein, then at Niederwampach, would have to get his striking force moved northwest to the Longvilly-Bastogne road - the smoothest route into town.

It seems altogether probable that the soaring ambition of this commander was responsible for his decision. He wanted to take Bastogne in person and the quick thrust was the only way to do it. He talked to some Luxembourg civilians in Niederwampach;

they told him that the side road through Benonchamps to Magéret was in good condition and perfectly feasible for the passage of armor. They said, "It looks bad but will get better and better." In this they misled him but the intelligence was enough to get him started. The road was narrow and deep in mud and became steadily worse. But no resistance was encountered and having started from Niederwampach at 2200, the force crossed the Luxembourg-Belgium border at midnight and reached Benonchamps one hour later. In the force was one battalion of infantry from the 902d Panzergrenadier Regiment, fifteen Mark V tanks and one battery of artillery, all under the command of the 902d Regiment's colonel, although Bayerlein went along in one of the lead tanks and appears to have personally directed the task force.

At 0200 the force reached Magéret on the main road. There a Belgian civilian told Bayerlein that two hours earlier an American force of fifty tanks and forty other armored vehicles under an American ma or general had passed through Magéret going east at about midnight. He was of course referring to Ryerson's scant force of tanks but the degree of exaggeration in the Belgian's statement was enough to offset all the damage that might have been caused by his disclosure. It shook Bayerlein badly and from that point on, the farther he moved forward the more he was constrained to worry about the security of his rear. Because he now knew that there was American armor operating along the Longvilly road between him and the German main body, Bayerlein set up a road block in Magéret composed of three tanks, some supporting infantry and a minefield covering the road from the east - the same roadblock that split Team Cherry and contributed so much to Ryerson's subsequent difficulties. The Germans at Magéret were certain that they could hear American armor moving around in their immediate vicinity but so dark was the night and such the confusion made by the slow movement of the last of their own vehicles into Magéret that they could not be sure where the sounds were coming from and hesitated to open fire for fear of hitting their own. The passage of this armored striking force onto the Longvilly road with the object of capturing Bastogne was regarded by the Americans who partially observed it at the time as only a "strong patrol action." It was so reported to Colonel Cherry and by him to Colonel Roberts. The Americans were still expecting the main enemy thrust to come straight down the main road.

At about 0400 the German force in Magéret began to draw fire from the near-by terrain. Though not greatly harassed, it fought back for about an hour and a half. At 0530 Bayerlein started his tanks on down the road to Neffe. As they worked their way cautiously along toward that hamlet they drew considerable fire from the high ground to right of the road. It is probable that this resistance came from retreating elements of the 9th Armored Division which had taken to the hills at the approach of the German column. The German force kept moving. The lead tank hit a mine at Team Cherry's roadblock just cast of Neffe and blew up; the Germans did not receive any fire from the Americans who had been manning the block and saw no signs of these men. So far not a shot had been fired and they got the impression that Neffe was undefended.

While the remaining mines were being cleared away from the road, one infantry company moved south of the tracks and advanced toward the Neffe Château. The company had no close tank support for the ground was still much too wet for armor.

So in this double-pronged fashion, the advance got under way again at 0550, with the armor (eleven tanks) riding the main highway. At 0700 the head of the armor reached the Neffe station and there it paused for almost an hour-an interlude that cost Bayerlein his one chance to strike Bastogne before Colonel Ewell could get started. All of the dash had gone out of the man by this time. There was no good tactical reason for the pause. But his own doubt about the situation stayed him. When the

244

order to proceed was at last given, the tanks advanced down the Bastogne road about 200 yards. Then they were struck by American fire. A machine gun in one of the leading German tanks had opened fire at about the same time. It was hard to say who had fired first. *[Here note that what Colonel Ewell had considered to be an enemy roadblock was in fact a striking force in motion.]* The German recoil was immediate. The loss to the German infantry from Colonel Ewell's opening fire was insignificant but the reaction among the foot forces was enough to deny the tanks the prospect of immediate support. The infantry wouldn't move and the tanks couldn't go forward alone. This deadlocked the advance for the necessary interlude. Then when Captain McGlone's battery went into action against the Neffe position an hour or so later, the impact was great. About eighty Germans were killed or wounded at Neffe within the first hour or so. Bayerlein, convinced by the sound (there was no observation because of fog and he was misled by the sound of the glider 105mm. gun M3) that he was being opposed by armor, retired to a cave near the Neffe station.

By noon, Bayerlein's mood was one of extreme pessimism. He had felt out the situation on his right and had found Colonel Ewell's left already advancing. Also, he had been impressed by fire that was coming at him from his left - the probable source of which was the small force of men under Colonel Cherry in the Neffe Château. He imagined that infantry battalions were advancing against both his flanks and that the battalion on the north was about ready to close in on Neffe. So he returned to Magéret, where the American tanks rolling back from Longvilly were continuing to hit against his armored roadblock. He passed through the village during the noon hour, some time before Ryerson's force really went to work against the block. His men had captured an American hospital in Magéret and he asked one of the nurses to look after his wounded. His nerve was working better now. He noted that the nurse was "young, blonde and beautiful." He no longer had any thought of pushing forward with his initial task force and he had about concluded that the capture of Bastogne would require the utmost effort on the part of his entire division.

It is now necessary to follow the course of the 2d Panzer Division through these same hours. That division was under orders to capture Noville as soon as possible. Having made the northward turn to the east of Longvilly, the point of the division advanced rapidly toward Bourcy, meeting no resistance en route. The small action at the Bourcy roadblock, although seemingly inconsequential, was sufficient to convince the division commander that he was blocked in that direction and that Noville was probably strongly held. He so advised the Corps commander and the course of the division was turned north so that Noville could be attacked from several sides. The men at the Bourcy block had mistaken this point for a "reconnaissance element" and concluded that they had made off after completing their mission. Instead, the block had changed the course of an entire division. There followed the heavy attacks against Noville on December 19 with the tactical results described earlier in the book. Its road temporarily blocked by this engagement, the 2d Panzer Division on the morning of December 19 was strung out along the road all the way from Noville back to the northwest of Allerborn.

By afternoon of December 19, Bayerlein, commander of the Panzer Lehr Division, had begun to feel himself harassed from every side and was thinking of extricating what he considered to be his "pocketed" forces. In his own words: "As to my own position, I felt that the resistance on my flanks would have to be annihilated before I could again attack. The movement of the infantry regiment which had come out of Bastogne to attack me had reacted decisively on my thinking. Their fire superiority at Neffe was something I had witnessed with my own eyes. I thought and said that we should attack Bastogne with the whole

XXXXVII Corps."

In these calculations, an overstrained imagination undoubtedly played a strong part. During the day, elements of Panzer Lehr (Bayerlein's reconnaissance battalion) covered on their south flank by the third regiment of Kokott's Division - the 39th Fusiliers of 26th Volksgrenadier - had pushed on toward Wardin. As we saw earlier, they had a limited success there and one of Colonel Ewell's companies of the 502d Parachute Infantry - Company I, on his extreme right - had been fragmented. But Bayerlein had eyes and ears only for the signs and sounds of enemy fire on his left, a state of mind aggravated no doubt by the activity of Team O'Hara's guns which had not supported Colonel Ewell's attack on Wardin but which were continuing to punish all enemy forces within sight or hearing.

Bayerlein, by his own account, gained the distinct impression that strong American forces had arrived in Wardin and were about to envelop his left; he could not conceive that the American infantry had been defeated there and that the American armor was preparing to withdraw to ground closer to Bastogne. The time had come, Bayerlein concluded, to direct every energy to the extrication of his force. But this was not easy to do. He felt that retirement by the narrow, winding road on which he had come - the road to Benonchamps - was now out of the question. If he were to make it at all, he would have to completely destroy and clear the American roadblock at Longvilly and move by the main highway. These were his thoughts after he had moved farther rearward from Magéret and he so reported them to his Corps commander, adding his personal urging that the plan be changed and that the entire Corps be thrown against Bastogne.

During these same hours, the XXXXVII Corps commander, Lieutenant General Lüttwitz, had received nothing but bad news from any part of his front. In sum, he had heard that Bayerlein had been stopped at Neffe, that parts of the 77th Regiment of the 26th Volksgrenadier Division had been stopped east of Bizory (by the 501st Parachute Infantry), and that the 78th Regiment of the 26th Division had been stopped at Hill 540, southeast of Foy (by Colonel Sink's forces). General Kokott, too, had expressed the same gloomy views as Bayerlein. He realized that the 101st Airborne Division had beaten him to Bastogne. And feeling that his own division might not be equal to the task of dislodging them, he urged that the entire Corps be committed to the task.

Lüttwitz reported to Fifth Panzer Army that each of his division commanders had gathered the impression that the enemy was in extraordinary strength at Bastogne. He added his recommendation that the original plan be changed and that the XXXXVII Corps be solidly committed to the reduction of Bastogne. Army refused the request, but it added a strange amendment to the previous orders. The Corps as a whole was given permission to renew the attack on a limited scale, since the position of the Panzer Lehr Division had become seriously compromised and so had that of the two northern regiments of the 26th Volksgrenadier Division. This was how matters stood on the highest level at 1600 on December 19.

But on the tactical plane, Corps and all three divisions bad been harassed mainly by thoughts of what might happen unless they destroyed the Longvilly roadblock. They had gone to work on that problem in early afternoon with such results that they should have become convinced they had reduced it to a cipher. The consequences to the American armor of the German attack against the Longvilly position on the afternoon of December 19 have been described earlier in their bare detail. But neither Captain Ryerson nor Lieutenant Hyduke had any idea then what major forces had been arrayed against them. In the course of the forenoon, out of Panzer Lehr, the 901st Panzergrenadier Regiment, one tank destroyer battalion with about twenty TDs, and an artillery battalion, had collected in the area of Benonchamps. Bayerlein, worrying about the Neffe-Magéret forces and the probable involvement of his reconnaissance battalion - the Panzer Lehr Division's reconnaissance training battalion - which had been shaken out farther to the south, seized on the Benonchamps forces to break the grip of the Longvilly block. Bayerlein did not realize at the time that a body of American armor was collected at the position which he was about to attack, for he had received principally mortar and small-arms fire from that direction. He bad already begun to discount the story told him by the Belgian the night before and was now swinging around to the idea that there was no American armor on his rear. This is the reason why he weighted his attack heavily with infantry. He ordered the force to attack from Benonchamps through the woods toward Longvilly, going east. Fifteen of the TDs were to give strong preliminary and supporting fires; the other five TDs were directed to accompany the two companies of infantry to the high ground. It was a trick, he said, that he had learned from opposing our 4th Armored Division in Normandy.

This assault force reached the top of Hill 490 a little time after 1400. From there, they saw the welter of American armor and motionless combat vehicles strung out along the Longvilly road, the tanks trying vainly to break away from their own trap. It was a target they had not expected at all, and it lay fully vulnerable at range of 1,500 to 2,000 yards. The other tank destroyers came forward. The twenty heavy guns of the TDs opened fire and so did all other weapons. (see map 27)

Nor was that all. To support Bayerlein's Neffe position on the right, Lüttwitz had ordered one regiment from the 26th Volksgrenadier Division to move to Bizory via the most direct side road. The advance elements of that regiment, the 77th, had already taken the road from Oberwampach going through Niederwampach. The rear elements were still within convenient reach to the southeast of the Longvilly block. Lüttwitz, not knowing of Bayerlein's action, met the commander of the regiment on the road between Oberwampach and Niederwampach and directed him to collect all artillery and

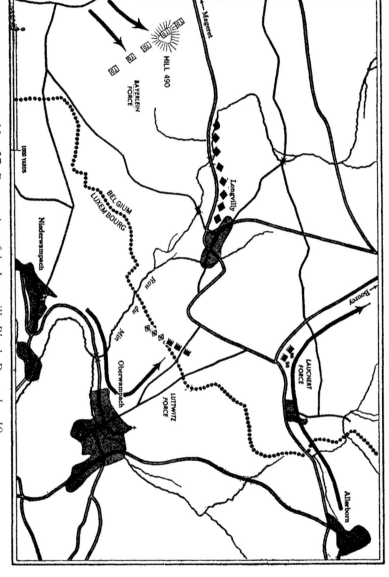

Map 27: Destruction of the Longvilly Block, December 19

heavy weapons in the general area and attack Longvilly from the southeast. He did so, and the force which went forward was heavy in antitank guns. By accident rather than from design it arrived at the high ground south of Longvilly simultaneously with the opening of Bayerlein's attack and its gunpower was added to the impact of the TDs.

Colonel Meinhard von Lauchert, commanding the 2d Panzer Division, had talked with Lüttwitz about the Longvilly block, but since his own people were turning north some distance short of the American armor, it hadn't concerned him overly in the beginning. But when he drew fire from the Longvilly direction (the action taken by the batteries supporting Hyduke) during the morning of December 19 and the shells threatened to interdict his turning movement, he directed that five or six 88-mm. guns be set up at the road junction below Chilfontaine to counter the American fire. This battery had been in operation for perhaps two hours when the two attacks were launched against Longvilly from the southeast and southwest. Its guns continued to fire and do great execution upon the stalled American column during the hours when the guns along the southern line were raking the armor point-blank. Here was surely the strangest passage in the whole enemy attack on Bastogne - all three divisions engaged at one time, bringing together the greatest fire concentration produced during the first phase of the siege. And their luckless target was a force which already felt itself defeated and was simply looking for a way out!

The bombardment lasted for about two hours, but even after that the German infantry did not close in. After Hyduke and his group fell back on Ryerson, who was trying to break through Magéret and so open a road of escape for what remained of the American force, some few American riflemen remained hidden amid the wreckage of the American armor and kept the enemy at bay with rifle fire - or at least that is the explanation of the German commanders. Dark was almost at hand when the

Germans moved out onto the road. Lüttwitz, fascinated by the spot, strolled among the riven hulls and noted that it was a strange place for a battle. This portion of the road was a kind of sacred way, lined on both sides with large stone crucifixes and a dozen or more heroic figures of saints. The burning armor was jammed in among these objects; the sacred images had served to block the way out. But Lüttwitz looked the tanks over carefully and concluded that Von Lauchert's guns had done most of the damage.

It was a melancholy night for Lüttwitz. He was under the impression that a strong American force had arrived at Wardin. And if that were true, it was a serious impingement on any effort to attack Bastogne from the south. His immediate problem was a kind of tactical monstrosity. He could use his entire corps against Bastogne and yet he had to commit it in such a way that there would be no chance of an involvement that would militate against the accomplishment of his basic mission to keep on advancing. He was dropping infiltration for the moment but he was not undertaking siege: there was no time to coördinate a general plan.

In the morning he felt a little better. Word came that Bayerlein's reconnaissance battalion (Panzer Lehr Division) had taken Wardin. Lüttwitz felt that this eased his situation, though no one bothered to tell him that Wardin had fallen into his hands without struggle because there were no Americans there. On the right the 2d Panzer Division took Noville somewhere near the middle of the afternoon, and again the Corps commander grew confident that the Americans were yielding to his superior force. He thought that an outflanking movement directed at Noville by the 2d Panzer Division from the northwest had brought off the capture of the village. He didn't know that the pressure on the American right rear had anything to do with it - a pressure coming from one of Kokott's regiments. Kokott's men had come through the woods and were pressing on Foy. It was this pressure that persuaded Colonel Sink to ask for permission to withdraw. So during most of that day Lüttwitz entertained an illusion that his hit-and-run effort was succeeding.

His hopes were again dashed by what happened to his center. The 901st Regiment, Panzer Lehr Division, tried for Marvie in the hours of the late morning and was repulsed. However, to Lüttwitz that was no more than an incident in the battle; he hadn't expected much. But when Bayerlein hit again from Neffe just after dark fell, and his attack was stopped cold, the whole command reacted gloomily. Again Bayerlein got a slightly exaggerated idea of the forces opposing him. "I was stopped by a tremendous artillery *[true enough]* and I also found myself opposing a great number of tanks *[not accurate]*. The effect was overpowering. We were stopped before we could begin." Again, to General Bayerlein the shock at Neffe was decisive. It also spelled failure for the Corps as a whole.

The Corps, meanwhile, had been extending westward to the south of Bastogne. When Lüttwitz heard that units of the Panzer Lehr Division had taken Wardin, he told General Kokott to take his reconnaissance battalion and the 39th Regiment, and swinging on a wide arc toward Sibret, make ready to attack Bastogne from the south. The advance followed the general line through Lutremange to Villera-la-Bonne-Eau to Hompré to Sibret but the roads on this line were so difficult for the armored cars that they had to advance well to the southward of the forest. Sibret was captured about 2000. The 39th Regiment reached high ground one kilometer north of Remoifosse and the wood one kilometer north of Assenois and there was brought in check, chiefly through the efforts of Colonel Harper's 327th Glider Infantry and the engineers. Having taken Sibret, Kokott's reconnaissance battalion went on to Chenogne, where it was brought in check temporarily.

Thus the Corps stood on the night of December 20, with Bastogne almost solidly in its embrace. On the south was

Kokott's 39th Regiment (26th Volksgrenadier Division). To the southeast, near Marvie, was Bayerlein's 901st Regiment (Panzer Lehr Division). And next to it, confronting Neffe, was his 902d. The 77th and 78th Regiments of Kokott were on each side of the railway running northeast out of Bastogne. Across the north, blocking all roads, were the elements of the 2d Panzer Division. That division was advancing to the west, and the extension of the general line, in so far as it was concerned, consisted only of roadblock elements whose mission was to protect the flank of the marching column.

Yet despite this apparently excellent situation of the Corps, Lüttwitz felt that night that so far as Bastogne was concerned, he was temporarily defeated. His chief subordinates, too, with the exception of Kokott, believed that the enforced continuation of the advance of the mechanized divisions to the westward, leaving the Bastogne assignment to Kokott's division, dimmed the prospect for a final victory. They had been impressed by the strength of the Bastogne forces and they felt that the task required unremitting pressure from the entire Corps.

In the course of December 21, Kokott's reconnaissance battalion got almost to the highway near Mande-St.-Étienne before being stopped by Colonel Harper's forces. The day was given over largely to the shifting of regiments as Kokott's division took over the general assignment which the day previous had been a Corps responsibility. Panzer Lehr was bound for Morhet. Bayerlein's 902d Regiment was replaced on the Bastogne line by Kokott's 77th, and his 78th Regiment took over the sector which had been held by the 2d Panzer Division. One regiment, the 901st, and some of the special elements of the Panzer Lehr Division were left behind, passing into Kokott's command.

On that day, also, the reconnaissance group of the 2d Panzer Division got only as far as Tenneville. Lüttwitz by now was devoting his entire attention to the progress of the 2d Panzer. He had wanted the reconnaissance group to move fast through the Bois de Bande and reach Bande by nightfall, but for some reason he couldn't get his lead forces rolling and the division strung out all the way from Tenneville to Bourcy. He found out later that the head of his column had been stopped by "strong enemy forces" maintaining a roadblock at a crossing southeast of Tenneville. This was, of course, the block maintained by Company B of Allen's battalion of the 327th Glider Infantry. It held up the progress of the 2d Panzer Division for one whole day, and of this delay much resulted subsequently. On December 22 and 23 the division pushed on only a little way; it was for the 2d Panzer Division a day of endless stopping, starting and turning, the sounds of which gave the defending forces within the Bastogne perimeter the impression that a tremendous enemy build-up was taking place to the north of them. *[The patrols into Rouette led by Lieutenant David E. White of 502d Parachute Infantry were in fact hitting against the outposts covering the flank of this withdrawing division.]* Again word came to Lüttwitz that the 2d Panzer Division's road was blocked by a stoutly held enemy roadblock. The report came from the same regimental commander who had engaged Company B, 327th, on December 21.

On the night of December 23-24, Lüttwitz went forward in person to examine the block. He received no fire as he came within range of it, so be rode on to the block and began taking the logs down. The block had been undefended throughout the entire time and the division had lost two days because of the hesitancy of this regimental commander who was subsequently court-martialed for cowardice. It cost the division dear, and not alone in time, for its vehicles were still strung out over these roads when the skies lifted and the American air strike came. Haltingly, and with other similar bad experiences, the division continued on its way toward Marche, Lüttwitz accompanying them.

Kokott, on taking over the main burden of reducing Bastogne, was at first flushed with optimism. On the morning of December 20 he had been at Wardin, where an American shell hit his CP truck, killed the other occupants and propelled Kokott against the wall of the village church. He was badly stunned; it was his closest call of the war. But he had been encouraged by the taking over of the position. After briefing the 39th Regiment and the reconnaissance battalion for the move westward toward Sibret, he went with them, to make certain that they moved as he wanted. So doing, he gained a first-hand impression that Bastogne was wide open on the south and west. He saw certain of the American elements which, either in moral or physical dissolution, were attempting to move south away from Bastogne. But what he saw he mistakenly interpreted. He thought these retreating fractions signified that the Bastogne defense was now disintegrating. This suspicion became a conviction when at Sibret he talked to a Belgian who assured him that the Bastogne garrison was falling apart. Arriving at his CP at Bras at 0200 on the morning of December 21, he was further cheered by the news that the 5th Parachute Division on his left flank (to the south) was making good progress. Kokott had found the roads very muddy, greatly choked by disabled vehicles left behind by both armies and frequently disturbed by artillery fire from within Bastogne.

The next two days were largely given over to maneuver, as Kokott's 26th Volksgrenadier Division extended westward in an attempt to complete the envelopment. The 77th Regiment was shifted to confront Bastogne from the northwest quarter; the 78th was to the 77th's left in the northeast sector; the 901st of Panzer Lehr Division still confronted the Marvie sector; the 39th Regiment was astride all roads leading into Bastogne from the southeast; the reconnaissance battalion had almost closed the circle on the west side and was moving toward the town from the southwest. On the west side between the reconnaissance battalion and the 77th Regiment, there was a small armored force from Panzer Lehr Division. But even so, where the road ran from Bastogne to Champlon, the line had not been rounded out. The American fire upon this artery was so intense that Kokott's forces could not gain the road, though they had it under such fair observation that they could interdict it effectively against American traffic.

For the time being, the 26th Volksgrenadier Division was sufficiently supplied with gasoline, having taken over some American stores during the swing through to Sibret. Mortar and artillery shells, however, were running short and this had become a drag upon operations. General Kokott didn't have the slightest suspicion that the opposing camp was plagued by the same problem. He noted that whenever the American artillery spoke, it did so in heavy concentrations. It was seldom that a single gun fired for in the interest of conserving ammunition there was little use of harassing fires. To Kokott's mind this suggested that the American artillery was being used with confidence and he reasoned that it must be amply supplied with ammunition. Heavy concentrations equal heavy supply: that was how he reasoned it.

Matters worsened on December 23. To the southward there was a near crisis when Kokott's rear began to feel pressure from the American thrusts northward to relieve Bastogne. Kokott's forces first became aware of the pressure when elements of the 5th Parachute Division fell back into their area. There were five newly arrived Tiger tanks near Kokott's CP. He didn't know where they had come from and he didn't stop to inquire. He sent them on down the Clochimont road in an effort to restore the situation. Soon after the German tanks departed, Kokott saw the first American troop-carrier planes come over on the Bastogne re-supply mission. He and his officers saw the parachutes dropping; they thought that additional paratroops were arriving to swell the ranks of the defenders. The effect was, as he expressed it, "to increase the disorder in the ranks of the attackers."

That night, on Corps order, he attacked Marvie, intending to smash through to Bastogne. The 901st Regiment was sent against Marvie, while the 39th Regiment, on its left, moved along the main road from Assenois. In an extension of this same line, forming roughly a half circle, the reconnaissance battalion, 26th Volksgrenadier Division, also moved to the attack and for the first time was able to close its grip on the Bastogne-Champlon road. The attack failed, as related earlier in the book. Kokott received early reports that his forces had "captured" Marvie *[an exaggeration]* but he never knew that the Panzer Lehr Division had broken the line at Hill 500 that night or that some of its tanks had entered Bastogne. *[Kokott's comment on this was: "They took only the first few houses and then reported to me that they had captured the village. I acted on the assumption that they were telling the truth. This is a very common type of error in our operations."]*

On the same night, while the Marvie attack was flickering, Kokott was visited at his CP by General Hasso-Eccard Manteuffel, Commanding General of the Fifth Panzer Army. An order had come down from XXXXVII Corps that Bastogne would be attacked again on Christmas Day and Manteuffel had come in person to give his instructions. By this time the German high command was thoroughly alarmed. The continued resistance at Bastogne and the southern action in support of it were holding up the advance of their entire Seventh Army. Manteuffel said it was necessary to hurry the conquest of the town because resistance from the south against the 5th Parachute Division was increasing hour by hour. He added, "Bastogne must be taken at all costs."

Manteuffel asked Kokott what he proposed and Kokott said that inasmuch as he had tried from every other direction and had taken heavy losses, he would now attack from out of the northwest. The 77th, which was the freshest of his regiments and had taken the least losses, was holding this sector. He reasoned, too, that the Americans would be looking primarily to the east and south and that their strength would be deployed in these directions, with weakness in the northwest. *[He was all wrong about this. The forces were strongest and freshest in the area he proposed to attack.]* His final argument was that the terrain in the northwest was the most favorable for the employment of armor, being relatively open and firm, so that the tanks would not have to be bound by the roads.

Manteuffel then agreed to put the 15th Panzergrenadier Division at Kokott's disposal and directly under his command for this attack. The division was only then moving up, a veteran division with considerable experience on the Italian front, and it would arrive in good condition.

The forward elements of the 15th Panzergrenadier Division reached the sector confronting Champs and Hemroulle about 2200 on December 24. There were immediately available two artillery battalions, one tank battalion (with about thirty medium tanks and tank destroyers) and the spearheads (two battalions) of the first two infantry regiments. For the troops of that division, it was simply a question of how many could get forward to the assembly area before jump-off time. Kokott bad decided that he had to attack in the dark because of American air superiority and be had set the hour at 0300 on Christmas morning. He reasoned further that his troops would have to be in Bastogne by 0800, for he felt that he would not be able to continue the attack advantageously after daylight.

The greater part of the first two regiments of 15th Panzergrenadier Division got forward in time to be fed into the attack, along with the tank battalion. Some of these men rode the tanks; others followed in an infantry line that wavered from the beginning, because its members had had little chance to catch breath or get their bearings after arrival at the front. Kokott's 77th Regiment attacked on the left against Champs, and he had the impression that this was the only part of the attack that got off strongly. His reconnaissance battalion, to the southward of the sector where the elements of the 15th Panzer Division struck against Colonel Harper's position, was also supposed to have joined in the attack, although this demonstration made almost no impression on the defenders. The troops confronting the eastern and southern parts of the perimeter were ordered to support the attack with continuing fires to prevent reinforcement of the westward-facing positions.

Thus the plans and intentions of the enemy in the Christmas Day fight. The results were as described in an earlier chapter. By 1000 Kokott knew that his plan was irretrievably lost. At 1200 he asked XXXXVII Corps for permission to stop the attack and reorganize. Corps refused, saying that it had become absolutely necessary to capture Bastogne, since the pressure on the south was becoming uncontainable. But the fight *[at the hinge of our 327th Glider Infantry-502d Parachute Infantry front]* had run its own course and was already dying. Kokott reluctantly renewed the attack, knowing now that the only effect would be to increase his losses.

MORE FROM THE SAME SERIES

Most books from the 'World War II from Original Sources' series are edited and endorsed by Emmy Award winning film maker and military historian Bob Carruthers, producer of Discovery Channel's Line of Fire and Weapons of War and BBC's Both Sides of the Line. Long experience and strong editorial control gives the military history enthusiast the ability to buy with confidence.

The series advisor is David McWhinnie, producer of the acclaimed Battlefield series for Discovery Channel. David and Bob have co-produced books and films with a wide variety of the UK's leading historians including Professor John Erickson and Dr David Chandler.

Where possible the books draw on rare primary sources to give the military enthusiast new insights into a fascinating subject.

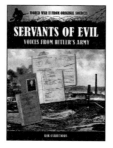

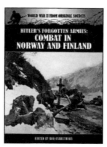
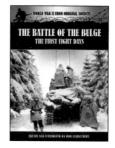
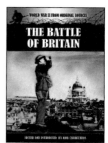

For more information visit www.pen-and-sword.co.uk